FALLING INTO WRETCHEDNESS
Ferbane in the late 1830s

Maynooth Studies in Local History

GENERAL EDITOR   Raymond Gillespie

This is one of six new pamphlets published in 1998 in the Maynooth Studies in Local History series. Like their fourteen predecessors these volumes illustrate, through case studies of particular areas and themes, how life in Ireland in the past evolved in a variety of settings, both urban and rural. As such they join a rapidly growing literature dealing with the local dimension of Ireland's past. That 'localness' is not primarily territorial, although all are firmly rooted in a sense of place, but derives from an awareness of the regional diversity of Irish society in the past.

Local history is not about administrative frameworks or geographical entities but rather about the people who created the social worlds which made particular places distinctive. These pamphlets are therefore primarily about people who lived in particular places over time. The range of people explored is wide; from the poor of pre-famine Drogheda and Ferbane through the nouveau riche world of the Meath grazier to the aristocratic lifestyle of an eighteenth-century Tipperary landlord. What all these people have in common is that they shaped their particular places in response to stimuli both from within their communities and from the wider world.

Like their predecessors these pamphlets allow us a brief glimpse into the diverse, interacting worlds which are the basis of the Irish historical experience. In their own right they are each significant contributions to our understanding of that experience in all its richness and complexity. They present local history as the vibrant and challenging discipline that it is.

Maynooth Studies in Local History: Number 15

Falling into Wretchedness

Ferbane in the late 1830s

Helen Sheil

IRISH ACADEMIC PRESS

First published in 1998 by
IRISH ACADEMIC PRESS
44, Northumberland Road, Dublin 4, Ireland
and in North America by
IRISH ACADEMIC PRESS
c/o ISBS, 5804 NE Hassalo Street, Portland, OR 97213
website: http://www.iap.ie

British Library Cataloguing in Publication Data

Shiel, Helen
    Falling into wretchedness: Ferbane in the late 1830s.
    (Maynooth studies in local history)
    1. Ferbane (Ireland) – History – 19th century 2. Ferbane
    (Ireland) – Social conditions – 19th century 3. Ferbane
    (Ireland) – Social life and customs – 19th century
    I. Title 941. 8'6

ISBN 0–7165–2704–9

Typeset in 10 pt on 12 pt Bembo by
Carrigboy Typesetting Services, County Cork
Printed by ColourBooks Ltd., Dublin

Contents

Acknowledgements

It is with gratitude that I express my thanks to the following people who facilitated and encouraged me during the course of my study.

To Professor Vincent Comerford and to the staff of the Department of Modern History, N.U.I., Maynooth, and in particular to Dr. Raymond Gillespie, who revealed a new vision of history to me. To my fellow students in the Maynooth M.A. class of 1992–4, for their support and friendship.

To the staffs of various libraries and archives: the National Library of Ireland, Dublin; the National Archives, Dublin; the Library, N.U.I., Maynooth; Offaly County Library, Tullamore and Ferbane.

To my friends and colleagues on the staffs of St. Joseph and St. Saran's Secondary School, Ferbane, and Coláiste Muire, Ennis. I wish, in particular, to thank Andrew O'Leary, Ferbane.

I would also like to thank my family, especially my sisters, Áine and Sarah.

Introduction

During the period of this study, the late 1830s, the town of Ferbane and nearly four thousand acres of land on the northern side of the town belonged to the Rev. Henry King, who had inherited the property from his uncle, John King, in the early 1820s. The aim of this study is to investigate how people lived in the area around Ferbane, with particular reference to the Ballylin Estate, during the latter half of the 1830s.

The King family resided at Ballylin House, which was situated in an extensive demesne, about one mile north of Ferbane. Around 500 people lived in the town during the late 1830s, with an additional 9,000 people inhabiting the three parishes of Wheery, Gallen and Tisaran. In 1837, it is recorded that the Rev. Henry King was the proprietor of fifteen townlands in the parish of Wheery, and census records show that in 1841 these townlands were inhabited by 1,573 people who lived in 271 houses.[1]

It has been argued that local history is not so much about a place – be it village, parish or town – as about a group of people. A community has been defined as 'a group of people resident in one place, engaged in mutually dependant occupations'.[2] The people around Ferbane depended overwhelmingly on agriculture for their livelihoods. This study shows that growing pressure on scarce resources such as land and employment meant that, as the 1840s approached, it was becoming less and less possible for local people to depend on each other. Another historian has argued that communities are 'groups of men and women who live together within a well defined geographical area and share common bonds and assumptions'.[3] The notion of common bonds and assumptions is not directly applicable in an Irish context where not all members of a local community shared, for example, the bond of poverty (or wealth), and in which extreme and divergent views were sometimes held on such matters as religion or politics.

The concept of studying 'the relationships between the different communities of interest in a locality'[4] is a more useful approach for the local historian in Ireland. It is possible to identify a number of communities of interest, some of which overlap, in the area around Ferbane in the late 1830s. Some of the more obvious examples are how the rich related to the poor, landlord with tenants, townspeople with country people, Catholics with Protestants, locals with strangers and farmers with labourers. Crime, which was considered a serious problem in the barony of Garrycastle during the 1830s, involved many different interest groups; the law breakers, the law makers and enforcers, victims of crime and all the local onlookers. The investigation of how different groups around Ferbane attempted to affect or influence each other, and to what extent they succeeded or failed, forms part of this study.

The dates to be covered in this study were chosen for a number of reasons. By concentrating on a limited period of time, mainly between 1835 to 1840, it is hoped that a more complete understanding of the lives of those living in or near the town of Ferbane can be gained than might be possible in a more general survey covering a longer time period. Any particular time in the history of a local community in rural Ireland has its own significance, but the late 1830s are important because they show communities that were shortly to face devastation. The conditions that determined how well or badly a local community would fare during the Famine years were being set in place during the 1830s. Even in the 1830s, some commentators in King's County could warn, Cassandra-like, of the disaster that was to come. The late 1830s were chosen, also, because there is a concentration of sources available for that period. These were generated at both local and national levels, and include such valuable sources as the Ordnance Survey six-inch sheets for King's County with their related name books, and Samuel Lewis' *Topographical Dictionary of Ireland*.[5]

Official census records for Ireland begin in 1821. Apart from population figures, information on housing, occupations and literacy can be obtained from census records in 1831 and 1841.[6] Parliamentary records are a rich source for the study of any local area in Ireland during this period. The Poor Inquiry (1836)[7] is arguably the most important parliamentary paper for the study of local history in Ireland during the 1830s. It includes details gathered from every parish in Ireland about many aspects of the lives of the poor. Although the poor people of Garrycastle do not speak for themselves, local gentlemen and clergymen (but not the Rev. Henry King) lay bare the plight of those at the lowest levels of local society. Numerous other parliamentary reports deal with a wide variety of issues such as religion, education and trade.

The problem of crime preoccupied both local and national authorities, and was frequently the subject of parliamentary investigation. Perhaps the most interesting report concerning the Ferbane area in this regard is one from 1834, in which correspondence from alarmed members of the local gentry and a long list of outrages were used to persuade the lord lieutenant to proclaim various baronies in King's County, including Garrycastle.[8] Detailed accounts of individual crimes are available in the police reports for each barony.[9] Official documents generated at local level include the records of the grand jury and of the poor law guardians.[10]

Eight boxes of documents relating to the Ballylin Estate are held in the National Library of Ireland.[11] The King family first acquired land around Ferbane in the 1760s, and the link was not finally broken until the 1930s, but the papers preserved in the King Collection are not a comprehensive representation of either the private or business affairs of the King family or estate. The haphazard nature of the collection means that it is impossible to build up an accurate rent roll for any period between 1760 and 1930, or to ascertain full details of income and expenditure at any particular time. Letters concerning financial, legal or family affairs cannot always be placed in a definite sequence or related to specific matters. Although the King Collection is disappointing in many respects it can be cautiously exploited, especially when it is used in conjunction with other material.

Other miscellaneous items from the King household survive, including a small diary kept by Mrs. Harriette King in 1838, and a notebook containing details of servants' wages between 1821 and 1837.[12] Many of the entries in the diary are short, dull and repetitive, but they offer an insight into the day-to-day life of gentry families in the area from a woman's point-of-view. With one exception only male servants are dealt with in the Rev. Henry King's servants' wages book. Presumably Mrs. King was responsible for female servants, but no record of her dealings with them survives.

Contemporary descriptions of places, people and practices are also available in newspapers, travel writings and commentaries written at the time. Wariness is required in dealing with most sources in these categories. Writers of the time had a stake in the society in which they lived, and sought to influence their readers through their work. Bias is easily detectable in most newspapers and travel writings of the time.

The community that existed around Ferbane in the late 1830s shared many features with other areas around Ireland at that time: rising population, subdivision of land, over-reliance on the potato, lack of employment, high rates of illiteracy and so on, but none of these pressures affected any two areas in precisely the same way. Every community has its own 'peculiar local circumstances [which interact] with wider national developments'.[13] The chapters that follow attempt to identify and examine the particular circumstances that affected the lives of local people in the area around Ferbane. The lives of ordinary people in a small community in a part of Ireland that in the 1830s was dismissed as 'dreary' by one travel writer,[14] should not be passed over as trivial. Chesterton's remarks on another local community have been quoted by more than one local historian;

> Notting Hill is a rise or high ground of the common earth, on which men have built houses to live, in which they are born, fall in love, pray, marry and die. Why should I think it absurd?[15]

A local study may illuminate but will not replicate national history. Finberg argues that local communities 'have every right to be considered as distinct articulations of the national life',[16] and he further states

> The history of a local community is not a mere fragment splintered off
> from national history: it deals with a social entity which has a perfectly
> good claim to be studied for its own sake.[17]

Without meaning to take away from national history, it could be said that
national history is often less than the sum of its parts. Writing about County
Longford in the seventeenth century, Gillespie makes a statement that is
applicable to any period in Irish history: 'Ireland will not be properly under-
stood until the local dimension has been more fully explored.'[18]

Local Landscape and Community

. . . land itself is much more than a location for events but is bound up with the nature of those events and with the nature of the society it supports.

E. Estyn Evans[1]

The landscape around Ferbane in which, during the 1830s, an increasing number of people sought to eke out a precarious existence, was described in some detail in two topographical works which appeared in 1837 and 1838.[2] The town of Ferbane lies on the banks of the River Brosna, within six miles of Shannon Harbour, where both the Brosna and, since 1804, the Grand Canal, meet the River Shannon, the great natural barrier between east and west. Ferbane is situated in the barony of Garrycastle, the most western barony in King's County, whose western side is bounded by the River Shannon. Bridges over the Shannon at Shannonbridge and Banagher facilitate communication between the two sides, and mean that the people of Garrycastle are more likely to be affected by conditions in Galway and Roscommon than other residents of King's County, which stretches eastwards across Leinster and, for the residents of the baronies of Ballybritt and Clonlisk, dips southwards into Munster (Figure 1). Close proximity to Galway and Roscommon did not mean friendly relations between people on either side of the river during the 1830s. Connaught men who crossed into King's County to buy potatoes or to look for work were not welcome in the Ferbane area at that time.

In the 1830s, most of Ferbane town was situated in the civil parish of Wheery (also called Killegally), but a small portion, on the south bank of the River Brosna, lay in the parish of Gallen. Adjoining these two parishes was the smaller parish of Tisaran. The territory covered by the parishes of Wheery, Gallen and Tisaran forms the main area under consideration in this study. Reference will also be made, at times, to the parishes of Clonmacnoise and Lemonaghan to the north of Ferbane, and occasionally to the town or parish of Banagher (Figure 2).

The River Shannon marked a definite western boundary to the area around Ferbane, but no distinct border can be traced to the north, east or south of the town. Most of the town lay on the northern bank of the River Brosna, but the fact that a small part of it lay on the southern side proved that the bridge at Ferbane formed a more effective link between the two sides than

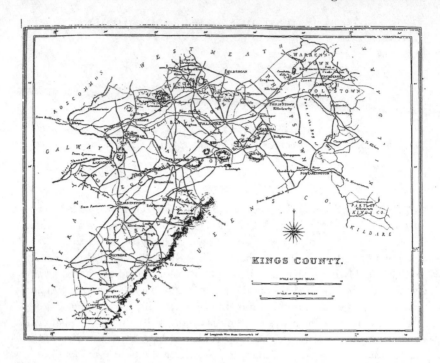

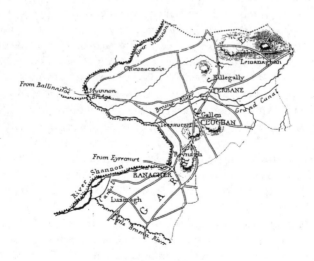

1. Maps showing King's County and the barony of Garrycastle from
Lewis, *Topographical Dictionary of Ireland*, (1837).

2. Map of civil parishes, townlands and villages around Ferbane. The King estate, 1837, covered the fifteen shaded townlands.

the river formed a barrier. A little further south, the Grand Canal, which had been excavated within living memory, was not an obstacle to community cohesiveness either.

Twenty miles away, in a south-easterly direction, looming low on the horizon, the Slieve Bloom Mountains could be seen, most days, from Ferbane. But in the 1830s, when the majority of people travelled on foot, and when individuals from only fourteen miles away were driven out as 'strangers', the Slieve Blooms were too far away to impinge on people's consciousness as any sort of geographical boundary. Eskers, which loop around the northern side of the territory around Ferbane, stretching roughly from Clonmacnoise to Moate, and other ridges scattered elsewhere throughout the area, were not significant delimiters of territory either. Esker ridges do not coincide with townland or parish boundaries.

By far the most distinctive feature of the landscape around Ferbane is the large amount of bogland. 'It extended on both sides of the road, as far as the eye could reach ... ' wrote one traveller through the district in 1834.[3] The Ordnance Survey, in its brief descriptions of each townland, provides information about the extensive boglands in the area around Ferbane.[4] Although many townlands contained useful or even good land, very few were completely free of bog. The amount of good land available in the 1830s was further curtailed by the fact that both the River Brosna and the River Shannon were prone to flooding. The Ordnance Survey recorded 'winter flood lines' on either side of these rivers on the six-inch map of the district made in 1840. Callow lands provided excellent grazing during the summer months, but there was little point in trying to cultivate them.

Most people living in or near Ferbane in the 1830s lived in a fairly restricted world. It is impossible to define a precise border beyond which people and places would have been regarded as not belonging to the Ferbane area, but it is probable that such a line would have been as little as six or seven miles away. Ordinary people, limited by how far they were prepared to walk, journeyed to fairs, funerals and elections. Fairs at Cloghan, Banagher and Ballycumber were frequented by people from Ferbane, even those only interested in carousing. Business led people further afield, to the fairs of Moate and Ballinasloe in particular. In 1837, a huge crowd from all over King's County attended the general election at Tullamore, but Tullamore, eighteen miles away, hardly figures at all in records local to Ferbane. Local men employed in 'horsing' goods up the canal to Dublin travelled on long journeys as often as they found work but, apart from this, it seems that among the poor only those who were emigrating, or who were involved in migrant labour or crime travelled long distances.

The Rev. Henry King and his wife, with a choice of horses and conveyances at their disposal, often rode or drove around the area for pleasure. Most of their outings were limited to places within a three or four mile radius of Ballylin, but they also went to Birr (where Mrs. King's sister was married to the second earl of Rosse), and occasionally to Athlone. The privilege of mobility, however, was not to be shared with the lower orders. In 1829, the Rev. Henry King discharged a servant 'for being absent several hours with one of my horses without my permission'.[5]

The countryside around Ferbane appeared beautiful to several commentators. Sir Charles Coote praised local scenery in 1801:

> The countryside immediately surrounding [Ferbane] abounds with the richest landscapes and finest prospects . . . The Brosna winds . . . through the most charming and fertile banks . . .[6]

Samuel Lewis, who relied on information provided by resident gentlemen to give what he questionably called 'a faithful and impartial description of each place'[7] described how Ferbane was 'pleasantly situated' on the banks of the River Brosna,

> . . . over which is a bridge commanding a beautiful view of the verdant plains and rich plantations through which it winds its course.[8]

Mrs. King certainly appreciated her surroundings. Returning from a six-week tour through England and Wales in 1838, she commented on the 'perfectly pure' air around Ferbane compared to the smutty atmosphere of industrialised Britain.[9] Beautiful countryside and clear air would have made little difference to Mrs. King's poor neighbours, living without sufficient land or employment in wretched sod cabins on the edges of bogs.

The landscape around Ferbane remained largely unchanged despite growing land hunger and poverty. There is evidence that a small amount of land was being reclaimed for agricultural purposes, but subdivision and monoculture, emigration and crime were more common responses to land related problems than back-breaking attempts to improve tiny plots of bogland which would then become assessible for rent.

Census figures for 1831 and 1841 provide a reasonable indication of population size in the area around Ferbane during the 1830s. Complete accuracy cannot be expected for a number of reasons. The census enumerators of 1831 were under the impression that their fees would be in proportion to the number of people recorded, so it is likely that numbers were inflated to some extent. The 1841 census has been praised as having 'a really high degree of accuracy',[10] but it has been strongly argued that it is a 'treacherous base' for population studies, particularly at local level.[11] Taken on a Sunday, it recorded 15 per cent of the total population of Ireland as 'visitors', and while this does not necessarily affect the national result, it could have serious implications in any attempt to analyse the results for a local area. Whether, or to what extent, 'visitors' distorted the result for the area around Ferbane is impossible to say, but they have been included in the following population figures for the area for two reasons: a native of one of the three parishes around Ferbane would have been termed a 'visitor' in either of the other two parishes and so rightly belongs in the statistics for the area. Secondly, while some non-locals, even if only from neighbouring townlands in the parishes of Clonmacnoise or Lemonaghan, were included in the Ferbane statistics, some local people would have gone unrecorded in the area because they themselves had gone visiting beyond the parish bounds.

Two other factors must be borne in mind when considering the population of any local area during this period; emigration and migrant labour. There is evidence that both emigration and migrant labour were taking place from the Ferbane area,[12] but the extent of each is impossible to quantify. The fragmentary nature of Ferbane parish records in this period means that they cannot be used to form a reliable birth register which might show the true rate of population growth during the 1830s. Connell gives numerous reasons why it would be 'fruitless' to attempt to discover what the population of Ireland would have been but for emigration.[13] The 1841 census commissioners themselves admitted that the figure of 58,000 seasonal labourers travelling to Britain that year was a 'considerable underestimate'.[14] It is probable, therefore, that while the figures given in the 1831 census are slightly too high, the figures given in the 1841 census are certainly too low, implying that population growth between 1831 and 1841 was greater than is officially stated.

Census results, such as they are, show that the population of Ferbane town, and of the rural area around it (comprising the three parishes of Wheery, Gallen and Tisaran), stood as follows in 1831 and 1841:[15]

Table 1. Population and number of families living in Ferbane and the surrounding area in 1831 and 1841.				
	Ferbane town		**Rural area**	
Date	*Population*	*Families*	*Population*	*Families*
1831	501	108	9062	1597
1841	537	102	11179	1997

It can be seen from these figures that while the town population rose by 7·19 per cent, the rural population increased by 23·36 per cent. Local clergymen and gentlemen, replying to a question about population trends in their areas in 1836, all made similar responses: 'increasing rapidly', (Gallen) or 'very much increasing' (Killegally/Wheery).[16] Despite the significant increase in the population of the general area, the town of Ferbane was not developing. There was obviously little in the line of trade or employment to attract people into the town even though the number of families trying to survive on a fixed amount of land had increased by over 25 per cent between 1831 and 1841. The growth in population meant that there was increasingly desperate – even vicious – competition for employment and land, while onlookers despaired as they watched conditions deteriorating all the time.

Ample evidence of the divisions between the rich and the poor was displayed in the landscape around the area. The large houses of the rich were situated in fine demesnes, with hundreds of acres devoted to managed wood-land, pleasure gardens and ornamental grounds. The townland of Ballylin in which the Kings had their residence, extended to over 583 acres. Apart from a small portion of bog, 'the principal part of it [was] laid out in ornamental grounds'. Moystown Demesne, 589 acres, the home of Col. L'Estrange in the parish of Tisaran, had 'stables, lawns, orchards and pleasure gardens'. Moystown House was a 'beautiful house . . . in excellent repair'. Meanwhile, in the only such emotive comment recorded for any townland in the area, the Ordnance Survey name books said that Col. L'Estrange's tenants in the townland of Clonbonniff lived 'miserably'.[17]

For the first time in the census of 1841, information was gathered con-cerning housing quality. Houses were divided into four classes. Houses in the fourth class consisted of one-roomed cabins built of mud or sods; those in the third class were little better but had two to four rooms; second-class houses were of superior quality with between five and nine rooms; anything better was considered first-class. Nationally, 40 per cent of houses were in the fourth class, and 37 per cent were in the third class.[18] The statistics available for Ferbane offer an insight into the structure of society in the area.[19]

Table 2. Housing quality, 1841				
	Ferbane town		**Rural area**	
	No.	*per cent*	*No.*	*per cent*
1st class	6	6·38	25	1·38
2nd class	24	25·52	432	23·78
3rd class	42	44·68	745	41·00
4th class	22	23·40	615	33·85

These figures show that the town area was more prosperous than the sur-rounding rural area with a higher proportion of first class houses and a lower proportion of houses in the fourth class. However, both shared similar proportions of second and third class dwellings. In the rural area, Wheery's housing stock was significantly worse than either Gallen's or Tisaran's. The number of fourth class dwellings in Wheery exceeded the number of third class dwellings. Over one-third of this parish was bog, a higher proportion than in Gallen or Tisaran. In Wheery, 41·67 per cent of houses were in the fourth class, and 35·53 per cent in the third class, which conforms fairly closely with the national averages of 40 per cent and 37 per cent respectively.

Cabins built on the edges of bogs were wretched in the extreme. Lewis, in his description of housing in King's County echoes an 1801 account by Sir Charles Coote:

> The houses of the small farmers are very mean, and the peasants' cabins throughout are miserably poor, in few instances weatherproof, and mostly thatched with straw; on the borders of the bogs they are still worse constructed, being covered only with sods pared off the surface, called scraws, or with rushes.[20]

Such houses were easily destroyed in disputes over land and housing. They were also easily robbed. In July 1839, five shillings was taken from a house at Bishop's Hill near Clonmacnoise by intruders who broke 'through the wall of the house which was made of sods'.[21]

There is some evidence to show that people who lived in the area around Ferbane in the 1830s regarded themselves as part of a 'conscious' community,[22] but the evidence also suggests that the idea of community operated at two different levels at least. The rich and the poor, although they inhabited the same general area, and were often linked by strong bonds such as the landlord-tenant relationship, lived very different and distinct lives.

Dotted around the countryside, the wealthy members of society shared certain characteristics; they were members of the Established Church, usually owned substantial tracts of land, and could be observed traversing the local area on horseback, or in gigs or closed carriages, paying each other social calls, perhaps carrying gifts of grapes from their glasshouses. In her diary of 1838,[23] Mrs. King's main theme is to list all the visitors who came to Ballylin House, and to record the local excursions made by herself, her husband and her children. Their circle of friends included many members of the local gentry – the Bagnals of Kilmore House, the Mahons of Killegally, Lauders of Moyclare, Mullocks of Bellair and Kilnagarnagh, the Dalys of Castledaly, and the Mooneys of Doon. The local medical doctor, Dr. Fry, and many Church of Ireland clergymen were also welcome guests at Ballylin House.

Although the Kings spent much of their time riding and driving around the local area, and must have seen for themselves how difficult life was for the poor, Mrs. King only twice referred to the poor, who constituted a large proportion of the population all around her, in the 1838 diary. In August that year, the Kings' land steward, Robert Nugent, gave them a 'miserable' account of the crops and said that the potatoes were so wet 'that the poor people can hardly eat them & find they disagree with their health'.[24] Despite the fact that the poor find so little space in her diary, Mrs. King was not uncharitable. Both in a threatening letter sent to King in 1837, and in her death notice in a local newspaper in 1847, references were made to her generosity to the poor.[25]

The poor were certainly discussed among the gentry class. Two close acquaintances of the King family gave what must have been their previously formulated joint testimony to the Poor Inquiry of 1836. R.J.E. Mooney, Esq., J.P., owner of some 4,800 acres, and Thomas H. Mullock, Esq., J.P., who owned some 5,200 acres, both lived in the neighbouring parish of Lemonaghan. They thought the poor were 'disposed to [be] idle', and that they 'could be much more comfortable were it not for their love of whiskey, politics and cardplaying'.[26] Illicit distillation had, in their opinion, become 'frightfully prevalent' in Lemonaghan, and was,

> injurious to the health and morals of the lower orders, makes them vero-
> cious, idle and unfit for labour of any kind, and in general urges them
> to the commission of crime, which, in their sober senses they would not
> be guilty of, *it is to be hoped*.[27]

Elements of frustration, as well as of distaste and prejudice are apparent in the attitudes of Mooney and Mullock. They evidently thought that it was impossible to improve the condition of the poor as it seemed to them that the poor were unwilling to help themselves:

> . . . neither do I think they would like the trouble of making themselves
> comfortable from the dirt and and filth they collect about their cabins
> and within them, and from their inattention to wholesome good advice
> given by persons who truly have their interest at heart.[28]

At the other end of the scale, it is clear that the poor had little to do with the rich. The poor were generally – though not exclusively – Catholic, lived lives of monotonous hardship, grew potatoes rather than corn, and, for those involved in illegal activities, committed crimes against their own kind. On the one occasion during the late 1830s when the Rev. Henry King was a victim of crime, the threatening letter sent to him began in a tone of obsequious respect, 'Reverend Sir, I cannot get over writing to your honour . . .'[29]

The evidence which survives about a sense of community spirit among the poor is negative rather than positive. Finberg's description of a set of people defining themselves 'in contradistinction from the many outsiders who do not belong'[30] is very apt. Much resentment of 'strangers', who were frequently the recipients of threatening letters or were the victims of attack, is evident in the police reports for Garrycastle in the late 1830s. A fast growing local population meant that basic requirements such as land, housing, employment and even food were in short supply. Poor outsiders, for example labourers from Connaught or a widow relying on the charity of her neighbours, represented an unacceptable drain on scarce resources to the local population. And so, the Widow Rooney of Clongowney, originally from Ballymoate, had her house pulled down and was threatened with death unless she left the area. A local man providing lodgings for Connaught labourers, who were employed breaking stones by a road contractor at Grogan, was sent a threatening letter, 'if you do not banish the strangers out of your house . . . you may prepare your coffin'; Mary Ryan of Clonlyon was ordered to dismiss a servant girl who was a 'stranger' in that part of the country. Over twenty Connaught cartmen who came to buy potatoes at Ferbane fair were beaten up as they returned towards Shannonbridge because their presence at the fair meant a rise in the price of potatoes.[31] Some outsiders did manage to establish themselves successfully in the area. Timothy Caman of Ballysheil received a threatening letter directed not against himself but against a lodger from Tipperary, warning him,

> not to keep the stranger . . . or if you do mark the consequence, you are a stranger here yourself and I order you not to put me to any more trouble, and if you do I will put you in the coffin . . . Tim Caman, do not keep this man here.[32]

The direct link between deteriorating local conditions and antipathy towards strangers was expressed in a letter sent by 'Captain Starlight' to Mr. L'Estrange of Moorock House, Lemonaghan:

> . . . I mention with feelings of regret the penury and perturbation the people are reduced to, all in consequence of allowing such detestable and vicious miscreants [i.e. strangers] to contaminate the soil where once superfluous hospitality dwelt . . .[33]

Even if this was a glorified view of the past it is true that a large part of the population around Ferbane in the late 1830s faced an uncertain future. The only valuable natural resource, land, was in many parts taken up by bog, and with no significant trade or industry in the locality, it was only the increasing dependence on potatoes that allowed a growing population to subsist at levels that sank lower as year followed year.

The Kings of Ballylin

The King family had been established at Ballylin since 1762, when John King of Fermoyle, County Longford, bought 247 acres of 'profitable land plantation measure' from the Armstongs of Gallen.[1] The Rev. Henry King, (1780–1857), inherited the Ferbane property from his uncle, John King, (1760–1820), a son of the John King who came to Ferbane in 1762. Estate records show that Henry King was involved in the administration of the estate well before the death of his uncle in 1820. In the seventy years between the 1760s and the 1830s, the King estate had grown to 3,922 acres covering fifteen townlands, including most of the town of Ferbane.[2] The Rev. Henry King also owned land in counties Roscommon and Leitrim, which was left in the hands of middlemen.[3] During the year covered by Mrs. King's diary, 1838, the Rev. Henry King did not visit Roscommon or Leitrim.

The land owned by the Rev. Henry King at Ferbane in the late 1830s cut across the centre of the parish of Wheery. A number of landlords lived in the vicinity of Ferbane, holding estates of several thousands acres each, but none was as well placed as the King estate. In a parish that was over one-third bog, King's land was concentrated on the better land. Using the crude measurements given in the Ordnance Survey records, it can be calculated that less than one-sixth of the King estate was bog. Another sixth was classed as poor land, but two-thirds of the estate was described as good or superior land.[4] King was also proprietor over nearly all of the town of Ferbane.

Records relating to the King estate[5] do not contain a complete rent-roll for any period in the estate's history, but some indication of the Rev. Henry King's likely rental income is available in the Ordnance Survey records. These show that in only one townland, Lisdermot, which was mainly bog, did the rent per acre slip below £1 per acre. These figures suggest that the potential rental income from the King estate in 1837 was over £3,500, excluding the incomes from Ballylin townland, the town of Ferbane, or King's land in Roscommon and Leitrim.[6] At this time, a labourer in the locality finding an average amount of work in the year, earned about £8–£10 per annum.[7] It is unlikely that King succeeded in collecting all the rent due each gale day, but landlord-tenant relations seem to have been tranquil. In a list of hundreds of civil bill ejectment procedures for King's County between 1827 and 1833 not one case concerned the King estate.[8] In a threatening letter sent to King in 1837, the main complaints were directed against the steward, and how labourers were employed and paid, not against King in his role as landlord.[9]

In 1841, there were 179 houses on the rural portion of the King estate, eight of which were unoccupied. In the 171 occupied houses lived 1,058 people, giving an average of 6·19 persons per house. In the Ferbane town area (in that part of the town that lay north of the River Brosna, in the parish of Wheery) there were ninety-one inhabited houses containing 515 people. The average number of people per household in the town was 5·66. Although King owned only 22·34 per cent of parish land, this area held 40·95 per cent of the parish population and 41·19 per cent of the inhabited houses of Wheery.[10] The fact that nearly half as many people again lived in Ferbane town as lived in the rural portion of King's estate suggests that his theoretical income was considerably in excess of £3,500 per annum in the late 1830s.

One of the few apparently unbroken sequences of documents in the King Collection is a series of receipts from the La Touche bank in Dublin giving details of the Rev. Henry King's investments in government stock between 1815 and 1851.[11] Money deposited in government stock presumably represented surplus cash which King could comfortably do without, at least in the short term, and shows that, financially, the Ballylin estate was very successful. Between 1820 and 1829, King paid £16,538 into government stock; the most saved in any one year was £2,911, in 1828. During the 1830s the amount deposited increased substantially to £24,490. The amount saved during the 1840s was only £18,748, and this figure was distorted by an unusually large deposit of nearly £6,000 in 1846 which was in the names of both the Rev. Henry King and Mrs. Harriette King, suggesting that this was Mrs. King's money. The pattern of savings dwindled to nothing during the Famine years, and the final receipt records a single small deposit of £247 in 1851. Unfortunately, there is no information about investments King might have made elsewhere, and whether or when these bonds were redeemed.

In the absence of a comprehensive rent-roll, or leases dating from the 1830s, it is not possible to give precise sizes of the holdings rented by King's tenants in the 1830s. Leases surviving from the 1820s concern parcels of land ranging in size from seven to twenty-one acres.[12] In 1836, King wrote in an account book that he had let the townland of Coole, comprising 539 acres of mostly arable land, to his friend, Mr. Abraham Bagnal of Kilmore House, for four years at £402 per annum, with a year's rent paid in advance.[13] Apart from Ballylin, Coole was the largest townland in King's possession. Bagnal kept most of the land for his own use, and almost twenty years later he was still in occupation of nearly the entire townland, with four other tenants holding little more than eight acres between them.[14] In answers to the Poor Inquiry of 1836, it was stated that the maximum farm size in Wheery was fifteen acres and that conacre was extensive.[15]

The conacre system, by which a labourer rented an acre or less of land from a tenant farmer on which to grow potatoes to feed his family, was condemned by local gentry figures because it gave 'great facility to the innumerable, early and ill-timed marriages occurring every other day'.[16] Rack rents for conacre were the norm, with an acre of potato land costing up to £9 in the parish of Wheery in the 1830s. Even though local landlords blamed the granting of conacre by their tenant-farmers for rising poverty in the area, they did little to resist it. Any attempt to curtail conacre would have been a major cause of agrarian unrest.

Mrs. King's nephew, the third earl of Rosse, writing about landlord-tenant relations in the first half of the nineteenth century stated that, '. . . on a large proportion of the estates in Ireland the majority of the tenants have not been of the landlord's choosing . . .'[17] Landlords' control over their estates in the area around Ferbane was affected in two ways: apart from the fact that there were already too many people from within the area seeking a foothold on the land, there was during the late 1830s, a widespread system of intimidation in operation. The nocturnal activities of 'Captain Rock' and his companions meant that in the relatively rare cases in which evictions were carried out, new tenants could seldom be found. It was for the same reason that consolidation of holdings in the area around Ferbane hardly ever happened, and then usually in cases where the previous tenants had emigrated, rather than been forced off the land. In evidence to the Poor Inquiry for the parishes of Wheery, Gallen and Tisaran, it was stated that no examples of consolidation had taken place within recent memory, for example, 'I know of no instance of the kind; the contrary practice prevails of subdividing large farms'[18] was the answer given for Gallen. Indeed, pressure was sometimes exerted on pastoral farmers to give up their land. In 1839, John Gorman of Gallen was prevented from mowing his meadow in an effort to induce him to 'give up the possession of the meadowing'.[19]

Even if the Rev. Henry King had little option in his choice of tenants, leases dating from the 1820s show that he did attempt to control their conduct. In a lease agreement for twenty-one acres of land at Kincor, including a mill and kiln, fishing rights and 'sufficient turbary for the use of the dwelling house & mill', made with John English of Lisdermot in 1821, certain obligations and restrictions were placed on the tenant. English had to dry and grind all the malt and corn required by the house and family at Ballylin free of charge. The buildings, water courses and equipment were to be kept in good repair. A penalty of double rent (i.e., £100 rather than £50 per annum) would apply if English sold or alienated his interest, and King was to have the power of entry and distraint if the rent was not paid punctually or the terms of the lease were broken.[20]

A clause prescribing severe penalties in the case of alienation of a tenant's interest in a lease was the most common feature in leases granted by King in the 1820s. However, alienation could and did take place with King's permission during this period. Robert Horne of Creggan rented seven acres in the townland of Ferbane from King in 1821. The lease was for twenty-one years or one lifetime (that of Horne's son, William), whichever would last longer. The rent was to be £15 per annum. Four years later, with the approval of the Rev. Henry King, who had a copy of the new lease in his possession, Horne sub-let the seven acres to John Keating of Cloghan for a period of one lifetime (that of Keating's daughter, Eliza Maria) or for a maximum of seventeen years. Keating's rent was to be £18 per annum, and he was granted rights to 'sufficient turbary in Creggan bog' by Horne. Horne himself gave up the original lease in 1832, long before it was due to expire. No reason was given.[21]

It is impossible to say whether it was standard procedure for King to grant leases to his tenants or whether the majority of them were tenants-at-will. Instability in land tenure in the years before the Famine was probably caused not so much by the lack of leases or the forced ejection of insecure tenants, as by the constantly growing population and subsequent pressure on land availability.

The threat of eviction was not, officially, an issue for tenants in the parish of Wheery. In the seven years between 1827 and 1833, only four tenants were subjected to civil bill ejectment proceedings in Wheery, and in three of the four cases the case was dismissed.[22] None of these cases involved the major landowners in the parish such as King, Armstrong, Gore or Mullock. During the same period only two cases were taken in Tisaran, neither of which was successful, and in Gallen only twelve out of twenty-two cases were successful. Although the threat of legal eviction was remote, unofficial evictions took place in the 1830s. For example, Michael Mitchell of Clonlyon was forced out of his house, the roof of which was pulled down in order to prevent him reoccupying the house, and shots were fired at him for not paying rent to his landlord, Charles Claffey. Dorah Owens and her children were forced out of their house at Lemonaghan and its roof was pulled down because she owed rent to John Bermingham.[23] Both these landlords were middlemen, renting land from the earl of Rosse and a Mr. Plunkett of Dublin, respectively. Other tenants were, at times, persuaded to give up their land without recourse to legal (or illegal) measures.

There is no evidence to suggest that the Rev. Henry King sought to influence the type of agriculture practised by his tenants, although from his many excursions around the area he must have known exactly what was being done or not done. During 1838, Mrs. King, who often accompanied her husband on his rounds, commented on the damage being done to grain crops and flowers by prolonged wet weather.[24] Evidence of improvements carried out by King is very limited. He agreed to bear the cost of building a dividing wall when he let a dwelling house and half the yard and garden at its rere to two apothecaries from Athlone in 1823, but when some industrious tenants attempted to reclaim a stretch of bogland they were dismayed to learn that King's steward was surveying the land, intending to 'bring them under rent for it'.[25]

Despite chronic underemployment in the area around Ferbane, King did practically nothing to encourage trade or industry in the locality. Attempts by one or two other landowners in the area to create opportunities for employment were the exception rather than the rule, and were usually doomed to failure. Colonel and Mrs. L'Estrange established a loan fund 'for the benefit of the industrious poor' in the parish of Tisaran,[26] but Mr. Thomas Mullock's ambition to develop a linen village at Bellair, earlier in the century, came to nothing.[27]

The Kings rarely patronised the shops or businesses of Ferbane, apart from a local butcher who supplied their meat to them even when they holidayed in Salthill in 1835.[28] In October 1838, they visited Pilkington's shop in Ferbane to inspect some building work, but were put off visiting Royston's inn because of the prospect of an encounter with the passengers of a 'car' which stood at the inn door. The only other time in 1838 that a shop in Ferbane was favoured by their presence was when the Rev. Henry King brought his children to visit William Bagnal's newly-opened shop.[29]

The Rev. Henry King employed a number of people to look after his business affairs. His banking was done through the La Touche bank in Dublin. Mr. Edward Piers of Lower Gloucester Street in Dublin was in charge of his legal affairs during the 1830s, and Mr. George Little of Birr acted for King as rent collector. However, the man who had most to do with the day-to-day running of the estate was the steward, Mr. Robert Nugent.

Nugent was hired as land steward to the Ballylin estate in 1826 at a wage of £40 sterling per annum plus board and lodgings.[30] Nugent was remarkable among King's servants for his longevity, which indicates that both King and Nugent were satisfied with each other's conduct. By 1837, however, resentment among the tenantry against Nugent had reached such a pitch that King was sent a threatening letter which had as its main complaint the activities of Nugent.[31] This letter is the only source to provide an insight into tenant attitudes towards the estate (see appendix).

According to the anonymous letter writer, the gullible King needed to be warned against a deceitful and avaricious land steward, whose conspicuous prosperity was based not on dollars from his son in America, as Nugent stated, but on fraud perpetrated against both landlord and tenants. Evidence of Nugent's wealth was given: he was building a house in Ferbane and 'taking ground'; he was lodging money in the bank; he had set up his sons-in-law as rich shop-keepers. At the same time he was threatening to bring a stretch of hard-won reclaimed bog 'under rent'; and was depriving the destitute of money given by King to be distributed among the poor for buying potatoes on market day. He had also allegedly terrorised some labourers into leaving King's employment to go elsewhere as migrant labourers ('to go into fairing country') and, as no proper tally of days worked was kept for each labourer, no man knew what wages was due to him any more than the 'beast that is in the field'.

The Rev. Henry King was himself reproached for paying the lowest rates in the neighbourhood. Other gentlemen paid 6½*d*. per day in winter and 8*d*. in summer, indicating that King's wages were very low indeed. The writer accused King of employing boys to do men's work at only 5*d*. a day. If these allegations are true it would seem that King's wealth was partly based on systematic exploitation of the poor. With only half of the estimated 424 labourers in the parish of Wheery in constant employment,[32] King and Nugent could easily find men willing to work for very low wages.

Even though death threats were made against both King and Nugent, there seem to have been no serious consequences. King continued to place his trust in Nugent, who was one of the few employees mentioned by name in Mrs. King's diary of the following year. Relations between landlord and tenant were not poisoned by mutual distrust and dislike, even in a part of the country which saw quite high levels of agrarian crime. A contemporary description of the damage caused to landlord–tenant relations in an area afflicted by crime – which the barony of Garrycastle was during the 1830s – seems not to have applied to the Rev. Henry King:

> A landowner in a county where the Whiteboy spirit prevails knows that he owes his security only to his means of defence, and sees in every peasant, even in his own labourers, a concealed or future enemy.[33]

From the evidence of Mrs. King's diary for 1838, the Rev. Henry King and his family had no qualms about walking, riding or driving unescorted among the local populance any time they liked. Excursions around the neighbourhood seem to have been their chief pastime. Mrs. King commented on many subjects: the weather, the state of the crops, the number of fatigued sheep being driven from west of the Shannon towards Dublin and Drogheda, whether her husband was happy with a particular horse or pony, but she never once expressed any doubts about their personal safety, and sent her children out walking and riding for the sake of their health. Her son, John, then aged sixteen, went out shooting by himself.

Ballylin House, designed by Richard Morrison, and built in a villa style in the early nineteenth century, was still, in the 1830s, a relatively new structure.[34] It survived the night of the 'big wind' with some damage to the roof, but many features of the surrounding demesne were destroyed, including an avenue of lime trees. Mrs. King thought 'it would require fifty years or more to make things look as they did before'.[35] Mrs. King devoted much attention to her flower garden, and had hot-bed frames and a glass-house. She also kept hens.

Many servants were employed at Ballylin House, but no records survive for the female servants who were probably under Mrs. King's charge. In her diary for 1838, Mrs. King recorded no details of the day-to-day administration of the household, and mentioned only three servants by name; the steward,

Robert Nugent, a cook, Walsh, and 'Miss C.', who looked after her three daughters. Details of the Rev. Henry King's dealings with the male servants have survived.[36] These show that apart from his steward, King also employed a coachman, a groom, a footman and, at times, a second footman, a gardener, and others known as 'in and out door' servants. Sobriety, honesty and personal cleanliness were the virtues most valued by King in his servants. Servants were dismissed for drunkenness, unreliability, because the King family was going on holiday, or, in one case, because illness prevented the servant from carrying out his duties.

Although the 1830s were years of rising poverty around Ferbane, and although there was quite a high level of crime in the locality, the Kings' lives were luxurious, secure and contented according to the evidence of Mrs. King's diary. Even in the threatening letter of 1837, there was no resentment about King's role as landlord, and animosity is directed, instead, against Nugent. Well-connected and wealthy, the Kings were lynch-pins in the society around Ferbane, providing extensive hospitality to their friends among the local gentry and Church of Ireland clergy, and also acting as landlord and employer to many people in the local community. The Kings were happy with their lives in Ballylin. On returning to Ferbane in 1838 after nearly seven weeks in Dublin, England and Wales, Mrs. King concluded her account of the holiday with an encomium to home:

> ... when we came home here ... the house & place looked in my eyes just as clean & neat as when we left it – if not more fresh and pleasant.[37]

Economic Life

For the poor people of Ferbane, life was neither pleasant nor easy. Agriculture was by far the most important activity in the area around Ferbane, but during the 1830s there was increasing pressure on the availability both of land and of labouring work on farms. Between 1831 and 1841, the number of families occupied in agriculture in the rural area around Ferbane, (i.e., in the parishes of Wheery, Gallen and Tisaran), increased from 1,284 to 1,499.[1] This meant that within a ten-year period, an extra 215 families had established themselves, however precariously, on a more-or-less fixed amount of land. In the same period, the number of families engaged in manufacturing and trade in the same area nearly doubled, from 140 to 276, although it is difficult to say what exactly these families were doing. Contemporary records give no indication of even modest levels of trade or industry in the area.[2] Despite the large rise in the rural population in the 1830s, the town of Ferbane conspicuously failed to develop. The number of families living there actually fell slightly (from 108 to 102) during the 1830s, and even within the town area over a quarter of the population was dependant on agriculture for its livelihood.[3]

By the mid-1830s the condition of the labouring classes was parlous in the extreme, with fewer than half finding constant employment, and when employed, poorly paid. Evidence given to the Poor Inquiry in 1836 shows that in the parish of Wheery only half of the estimated 424 labourers were in constant employment, with the rest finding work only occasionally. In Gallen, a mere eighty out of 450 labourers had fulltime work. The number of labourers in Tisaran was variously given as 130, 142, and 391, showing that not all respondents defined 'labourer' in the same way. Some labourers had small farms which they paid for directly through labour for their landlord or with money earned from labouring elsewhere.[4] Landlords such as the Rev. Henry King probably provided regular employment for several dozen labourers, but subdivision of farms in the locality meant that, as time went on, there were fewer and fewer large tenant farmers providing employment in the area. The 'hurried' times of the year (spring, harvest and turf-cutting seasons) were the only times in which most labourers found work. These were the only times, too, that women and children were employed, though at much lower rates of pay than their menfolk. The type of work occasionally done by women was 'dropping potatoes, spreading turf, binding corn and picking potatoes', according to one answer given to the Poor Inquiry for the parish of Killegally (Wheery).[5]

Labouring men earned 8*d*. per day in summer and 6*d*. per day in winter without diet, which would have been valued at 2*d*. During 'hurried' times wages rose as high as 1*s*. per day, but there would have been few such days available in the year. Women and children employed at busy times earned only 4*d*. per day without diet. The parish priest of Ferbane said that women and children earned so little so rarely that they were 'incompetent to provide themselves with proper clothing'.[6] Methods of payment varied somewhat. Some labourers were working off the rent owed for their conacre plots, others were paid in cash, but in Killegally (Wheery) it was alleged that labourers were paid 'in every way and any way, rather than cash', being forced to accept provisions or wool at above market prices.[7]

The lack of employment available locally meant that some labourers resorted to migrant labour, although it is impossible to quantify the number of people leaving the area each year in search of work elsewhere. Fr. O'Farrell, the parish priest of Ferbane, said,

> those having but occasional employment would be unable to maintain their families unless by seeking employment in other places.[8]

In the parish of Gallen, some labourers were reduced to living on 'the bounty of their neighbours' when they were out of work.[9]

Earlier in the century, the barony of Garrycastle was said to 'abound with linen manufactures'.[10] Ordnance Survey records show that there was a linen factory and a flax mill in the area. A hill in Lisaniska (Tisaran) was known as Bleach Hill 'from the circumstance of the people of this part of the country bleaching linen etc. on it'.[11] But even then the linen industry in King's County was much reduced compared to previous times. A linen output of £50,000 for King's County in 1760 had fallen to £20,000 in 1816,[12] and by the 1830s the linen industry around Ferbane was in irretrievable decline. The income derived from linen had encouraged the proliferation of small farms, but as the linen industry gradually collapsed these families were reduced to absolute penury. The Poor Inquiry commissioners were told of how the local population was suffering as a result of the decay of the linen industry:

> . . . numbers [of the poorer classes] were formerly employed in the linen trade, which is now at an end in this parish; they have no employment at present, and the farmers are unable to employ them . . . [Gallen].
>
> The condition of the poor has become wretched in the extreme these years back: the linen trade flourished in the parish, and the poor were then employed and comfortable; the decay of the trade has entailed consequent misery on its followers. [Lemonaghan][13]

Contracts for building and repairing roads given by the local Grand Jury were of little if any benefit to the labouring poor. For example, grants totalling £323.14s. 2d. were made at Belmont Petty Sessions in January 1838 for the repair of roads, walls, bridges and ditches,[14] but it is doubtful if any of this money found its way into the pockets of the poor. The contracts were monopolised by local farmers who, sparing expenses, did the work themselves with the help of their sons and using their own horses, giving little or no work to the poor labourers who needed it most.[15] In the few cases where labourers were employed they were often paid in an exploitative fashion. In Gallen, labourers were 'frequently paid in provisions at a very high price', and, in Tisaran, pay was issued in the form of orders on shopkeepers and oatmeal-makers who sold goods at 'exorbitant prices'.[16]

The building of the Grand Canal, which reached Shannon Harbour in 1804, should have been a boost to trade in the area around Ferbane, but even in its early days, well before the arrival of rail transport in Ireland, it was condemned as a white elephant:

> The Grand Canal . . . meets the Shannon too soon, and ought to have taken a southerly direction . . . the communication is so tedious and so bad, as to be little used . . . it does not even pay its expenses.

The same author's dismissive comment that it was '. . . characteristic of the Irish to cut a canal in the expectation of trade, rather than to wait until trade demands it'[17] seems to have been true in respect of the Grand Canal in west Offaly. By the late 1830s travellers could avail of regular services from Shannon Harbour to Dublin, Limerick and Ballinasloe, although better-off passengers from the Ferbane area avoided the canal in west Offaly by travelling to Kilbeggan on horseback to catch the fly-boat to Dublin.[18] The Rev. Henry King and his family never used the canal, preferring to travel by road to Dublin, even if it meant stopping overnight. Emigrants from the Ferbane area used the canal on the first step of their journeys. Police reports for the late 1830s describe how the police patrolled the canal banks every evening to preserve the peace as emigrants embarked for America.[19] A number of local men found employment from time to time 'horsing' goods to Dublin, but the number of crimes directed against non-local horsemen and boatmen, and against the canal itself, show that local people felt that they were not bene-fitting adequately from the canal.

Crimes such as cutting the banks or throwing stone blocks into the locks were intended to create work for locals who would be employed to rectify the damage. Crimes against the canal occurred all along the canal, east and west of Ferbane, but particularly in the stretch between Ferbane and Shannon Harbour, with outrages recorded during the late 1830s at Gillen, Belmont, Clonony and Shannon Harbour.[20] The Grand Canal Company offered extraordinarily high rewards in an attempt to find out the perpetrators of crimes against the canal. In August 1839, rewards totalling £220 were made available for information about the malicious cutting of the canal bank at Terraune, which caused the water level in the canal to drop by three feet over a length of seven and a half miles.[21]

The Grand Canal Company made unsuccessful efforts to promote trade in the area around Ferbane in an attempt to increase the volume of traffic on the canal. The Grand Hotel at Shannon Harbour, built by the company at a cost of £200, had a chequered history to say the least.[22] In the mid-1820s it was hoped to establish a market at Ferbane. The directors of the Grand Canal were advised to advertise the market in local papers and on handbills to be displayed in the adjoining countryside. They were recommended '. . . to give a small allowance or drawback for a limited time, to those who bring coin, purchase there & forward it in boats from Gillen Harbour.'[23] The Rev. Henry King was to be paid to waive his right to charge tolls and customs.

In 1801, it was stated that although Ferbane had a patent for a weekly market, none was held.[24] Later records state the opposite; a market was held every Thursday, but no patent was recorded.[25] In the early 1840s, no tolls or customs were collected at Ferbane fairs, and so it seems that the Rev. Henry King either could not or did not establish the right to charge tolls and customs.[26] The amount of trade carried on in the weekly market is impossible to assess. Potatoes were an important commodity, which at times, attracted unwelcome buyers from across the Shannon. An influx of outside buyers could raise the price of potatoes, and police protection had to be given to Connaught men buying potatoes in Ferbane in May 1839.[27] Evidently, local people felt justified in resorting to violence to maintain an exclusive right to whatever potatoes were available, and at the lowest possible price. During the late 1830s, the Rev. Henry King regularly donated money with which poor people could buy potatoes.[28] Wheat was also sold at the Ferbane market and was transported up the Grand Canal to Dublin. In 1838, there was an incident in which local people stole back twenty to thirty barrels of wheat which were being stored at Gillen, but which had not been paid for.[29]

Fairs were held in Ferbane twice a year, on 2 August and 20 October, but the September fair in Banagher and the October fair of Ballinasloe were much more important than the fairs which took place in Ferbane. Mrs. King, in 1838, remarked on the huge numbers of sheep and cattle being driven eastwards from the Ballinasloe fair.[30] Some of these flocks of sheep were kept overnight in the area around Ferbane, and with a value of up to £2 each, they were sometimes a tempting target for thieves.[31] Otherwise, the Ferbane area did not benefit from this trade between the east and west of Ireland.

The range of shops in Ferbane during the late 1830s was probably quite limited. Many poor people would rarely have visited shops, as they subsisted on their own produce. Shopkeepers were often resented by the poor, as some of them colluded with local farmers in exploiting the payment system to local labourers. One of the proofs of Robert Nugent's iniquity, in the threatening letter sent to King in 1837, was that he had set up his sons-in-law as 'rich shopkeepers'. Shopkeepers relied on the custom of those in the middle layers of society, as the local gentry figures rarely, if ever, went shopping in Ferbane. Mrs. King mentions only two occasions in which she or her husband visited shops in Ferbane in 1838, and neither time does it seem that any money was spent.[32]

During 1838, Mrs. King went shopping to Birr and Athlone, but the needs of the King household were brought there directly, or ordered from Dublin. At the end of Mrs. King's diary there is a long list under the heading 'Things brought here', and it includes many varieties of fruit, fish, poultry and game-birds, as well as honey, beef, bread and eggs. Ballylin House had a wine cellar, which was remodelled in 1832, with different sections for port, madeira, claret and so on.[33] A holiday in Galway, in 1835, was used as an opportunity for the Rev. Henry King and his son to acquire new items of clothing such as silk coats, jackets, trousers and gloves.[34] Various tradesmen, both local and non-local, did business at Ballylin House. Twice during 1838 a pedlar called with 'many nice books', and a Mr. Southwell came to tune their pianos. Slates were ordered, which were transported to Ferbane on the Grand Canal, and a carpenter was employed to make a horse block for the Rev. Henry King. However, when one of the britzka wheels broke, the coachman was sent to Dublin with it, to get it repaired.[35] Ferbane had a post-office during the mid-to-late 1830s, but no bank or pawnbroker. The only businesses which seemed to flourish during this period were public houses, of which there were forty-seven in the parishes of Gallen, Tisaran and Killegally (Wheery), in 1836, as well as six other unofficial establishments which paid no duties.[36]

It is clear that during the 1830s, the town of Ferbane failed to develop despite a rapidly growing local population. Unlike, for example, Clara, where in the 1830s, tobacco, soap and candles were manufactured, and where there was a brewery, tanyard, extensive bleach green, and four corn and flour mills,[37] Ferbane proved incapable of providing a reasonable level of employment or prosperity to many of its inhabitants. The local resident gentry did little to encourage trade or industry in the area. As the population increased during the first half of the nineteenth century, poverty became entrenched in the local community, so that by 1836, the parish priest of Ferbane stated that farmers as well as labourers had 'fallen into wretchedness'.[38]

Poverty

The state of the labouring poor, as well as of the farming classes, has lamentably fallen into wretchedness; the farmers, burdened by high rents and bad prices etc., are unable to employ or pay the labourer, who is consequently dragging a weary existence, deprived not merely of the comforts, but sometimes suffering under the want of nourishing sustenance.

Rev. P. O'Farrell, P.P., Ferbane, 1836.[1]

Fr. O'Farrell's description of poverty in the area around Ferbane in the mid-1830s could, with local variations, have been repeated in many parishes in Ireland at the time. The holding of the Poor Inquiry in 1836, and the passing of the Poor Relief (Ireland) Act in 1838, showed that the problem of poverty in Ireland had become so severe that it could no longer be ignored. As destitution increased during the first half of the nineteenth century, the pressure of 'continuous poverty'[2] meant that the poor could no longer rely on each others' support during times of distress. Although landlords strongly opposed the expense of an Irish poor law, and government officials feared the risk of encouraging the poor to become dependant on the state,[3] high levels of crime in Ireland meant that some commentators recommended that there should be 'legal provision' for the poor.[4]

During the 1830s, conditions in Ferbane verged, at times, on famine. In 1830, bad weather and flooding caused considerable distress in the area. There were reports of deaths from fever, and a local priest wrote to the Rev. Henry King, who was on holiday in Wales, appealing for help:

> . . . it is with . . . reluctance I am now prevailed on by suffering humanity to inform you that hundreds of the peasantry here are in a state bordering on starvation for want of food or the means of procuring it . . .[5]

In 1838, prolonged wet weather meant that potatoes were practically inedible and damaged people's health.[6] Even in relatively good years the lives of the poor were miserable. Records giving details of housing conditions, furnishings, clothing and diet of the poor show abysmally low standards for a large portion of the local population.

In the rural area around Ferbane (in the parishes of Wheery, Gallen and Tisaran), 33.33 per cent of houses were identified as one-roomed mud-cabins;

23·40 per cent of the town's housing stock was in the same category.[7] Rent for these tiny, rain-sodden hovels varied between 15s. and £3 per annum, without land.[8] Within these cabins, furniture was either non-existent, or 'so wretched as not to deserve the name'.[9]

Clothing was extremely poor among the labouring classes around Ferbane. Children were 'miserably clad' until they could earn the price of their own clothes. Although clothing in Tisaran was described as 'in general, pretty good', that of labourers in the parish of Wheery was,

> . . . so very bad, that they are unable in many instances, to attend to religious duties, or to be protected against the inclemency of the weather.[10]

The rags which were worn during the day were used at night as bedclothes. Even small items of clothing were regarded as valuable assets. When Mary Wilson of Cloghan reported that she had been robbed in 1839, she mentioned the loss of a handkerchief and lace cap as well as of money to the police.[11]

Potatoes dominated the diet of labourers. Evidence given for the parishes around Ferbane states that labourers mostly ate potatoes and salt, with perhaps, stirabout during the summer months when potatoes were in short supply. A little milk or buttermilk was consumed during the summer, and meat of an inferior nature was eaten maybe twice a year.[12] It was reckoned that a labourer's yearly expense in food should have been about £10, but it cost much less to live almost exclusively on potatoes;

> As labourers are now fed, it would take £3 or £4 for their scanty support, which hardly enables them to undergo their labourious engagements.[13]

The monotonous diet of labourers was in sharp contrast to the luxurious and varied diet enjoyed by local gentry families. A list of provisions brought to Ballylin House in 1838 included such exotic delicacies as oranges, lemons, lobsters and oysters, honey, and many varieties of fruit, fish, fowl, eggs and bread.[14]

Long before the Great Famine, it was known that potatoes were an unreliable crop. Evidence given to the Poor Inquiry for the nearby barony of Clonlisk condemned over-reliance on potatoes for several reasons:

> The potato being the principal food of the peasantry, and no plan having ever been practised here to preserve the surplus of an abundant crop, to meet the possible failure of the crops of succeeding years, they are each year dependant for subsistence upon the produce of that crop, and always suffer distress proportional to the extent of the failure . . . Potatoes are so bulky an article that they are often dear in one district, while they are cheap in a neighbouring one.[15]

Although corn would have been easier to store and transport, those who were most vulnerable to the vagaries of potato production could least afford the change to corn, which would have required more land, grinding fees to a local mill and 'kitchen' facilities at home.

Contemporary sources show that the poor were often blamed for their own privations. A midland newspaper of conservative ilk stated that the 'lawless and turbulent conduct' of the poor had 'banished prosperity from the land'.[16] Some local gentry figures thought that the labouring classes were characterised by idleness and over-fondness for whiskey politics and card-playing.[17] The poor were said to prefer their leaking sod cabins to houses built of stone and slate,[18] and to be inattentive to 'wholesome good advice' given by persons who claimed to have their interests at heart.[19] The apparent futility of trying to help the needy meant that the wealthy members of society could self-righteously condemn the fecklessness and ingratitude of the poor, and ignore their own role in the creation and perpetuation of poverty in the area. In 1837 the Rev. Henry King regularly distributed money with which the poor people of Ferbane could buy potatoes at the weekly market. Yet, simultaneously, he paid the 'smallest hire' (at only 5*d*. a day) in the local area.[20] Relatively wealthy tenant farmers kept road repair contracts to themselves, and paid their labourers 'in every way and any way, rather that cash'[21] much to the disadvantage of the labourers.

It is said that there was much 'spontaneous giving' among the poor,[22] and there is some evidence that poor people around Ferbane were reduced, at times, to relying on each other for support. Unemployed labourers in Gallen lived 'on the bounty of their neighbours' in the mid-1830s,[23] but relentless distress in large sections of the community meant that, as time went on, the poor were less and less able to help themselves. Police reports on cases involving petty crime and intolerance of 'strangers' in the locality reflect growing tension as a result of poverty in the area. Disputes between neighbours and even between members of the same family over property or land were probably motivated as much by poverty, or fear of poverty, as by greed. When Anne Lynch of Bracca lay dying of fever in 1839, she was robbed of her store of potatoes by family members who, according to the police, considered themselves entitled to a share of her property.[24]

Before the introduction of the Poor Relief (Ireland) Act in 1838, and the subsequent formation of the poor law unions, there was little formal assistance available to the poor. The establishment of societies to help the poor depended very much on local initiative. The Moate Protestant Benevolent Society, set up in 1836, was intended to ameliorate the 'truly deplorable' condition of poor Protestants in Moate.[25] No such organisation seems to have existed in the Ferbane area in the late 1830s. Private individuals gave help to the poor, but it is impossible to say how much or how often assistance was offered. The Rev. Henry King regularly distributed money for potatoes during the late 1830s.

Some years earlier, the parish priest of Ferbane, in a letter to King, acknowledged the 'obligations already conferred on the people of this parish' by King.[26]
The role of Fr. Keogh (and his successors) in soliciting aid from local gentry
figures was important in securing larger donations than usual at times of particular distress. At a time when there were few avenues of recourse available,
Fr. Keogh had to be careful to retain the Rev. Henry King's goodwill. It was
only when he perceived that the poor were bordering on starvation that he
resorted, with reluctance, to a direct appeal for aid in 1830.

Emigration from the Ferbane area during the 1830s was not particularly
heavy despite the fast growing population and the lack of employment and
land. In the parish of Wheery, which included most of the town of Ferbane,
the population rose from 3,054 in 1831, to 3,841, and it was estimated that
only ten or twelve persons a year were emigrating in the mid-1830s. About
fifteen people a year emigrated from Gallen, whose population rose from
3,976 to 5,309 in the ten years between 1831 and 1841. In Tisaran it was stated
that ten or twelve families had left since 1830 from a population that hardly
changed between 1831 and 1841, going from 2,031 to 2,029.[27] North America
was the destination of most emigrants from Ferbane. Most of those who emigrated were not at the bottom level of society. The families who left Tisaran
had been in 'good circumstances' and were 'chiefly Protestants' who sold their
interest in farm land around Ferbane in order to buy land in America.[28]
Robert Nugent, King's land steward, whose conspicuous wealth was deeply
resented by certain people, had a son in America who allegedly sent him
plenty of money.[29]

If poverty was not driving people away from the area around Ferbane, it
was feared by some local figures in authority that high levels of crime were
responsible for emigration. In 1834, it was stated that the 'loyal and peaceable
inhabitants' of Garrycastle barony would be 'ruined, murdered or obliged to
emigrate' if stronger measures were not taken against crime in the area.[30] This
was alarmist rhetoric, but five years later, at one of the first meetings of the
poor law guardians of the Parsonstown Union, another matter of law-and-
order exercised the minds of the powers that were in attendance. At that meeting, which was held on 28 December 1839, it was unanimously agreed that
pauperism should be criminalised. The Parsonstown guardians recommended
to the commissioners in Dublin that a clause be inserted in the Poor Law Act
'making mendicancy and vagrancy penal'. Although a letter was received from
the Dublin office 'entirely' agreeing with this resolution, it was withdrawn at
a later meeting in Parsonstown.[31]

Ferbane lay in the Parsonstown Union area, and some local landowners
were selected as ex-officio guardians. These included Robert Lauder,
R.J.E. Mooney, Andrew Armstrong and J.P. Armstrong. The Rev. Henry King
did not involve himself in public affairs because of his clerical status. The
Parsonstown guardians agreed to build a workhouse to accommodate 1,100

'destitute poor persons', but decided to complete work initially on a smaller unit designed to cater for 800 people. The first stone was laid on 23 April 1840.[32]

Although the poor law reforms of the late 1830s marked a radical change in official policy, with the government now accepting some responsibility for the care of the poor, the problem of poverty in Ireland was not solved. The poor law guardians had discretion over who was granted relief and nobody had a statutory right to relief.[33] The poor law system was certainly not designed to cater for the crisis of the late 1840s, although it is not only with the benefit of hindsight that the Great Famine can be foreseen. The problem of poverty in Ireland seemed intractable to some commentators in the 1830s, and in King's County at least one contemporary looked to the future with despair:

> ... the great mass of the labouring population are little removed from starvation. Out of this condition they cannot raise themselves ... if an immediate and effectual remedy be not now applied, a heap of misery is likely to be generated ...[34]

Crime

Belmont, a small village three miles west of Ferbane, was where the local petty sessions were held during the 1830s. In February 1834, the Belmont magistrates, alarmed by what they saw as a recent upsurge in violence within their jurisdiction, set down a series of resolutions which, later that year, resulted in various baronies of King's County (including Garrycastle) being declared to be in a 'state of disturbance and insubordination' by the lord lieutenant of Ireland.[1] It was stated that 'an organised system of robbery, outrage, intimidation and murder' had become established, and that of the sixteen outrages that had been committed in King's County in October 1833 fourteen had occurred in Garrycastle.[2] George Cornewall Lewis, in his contemporary account of crime in Ireland, used a long list of crimes committed in Garrycastle during March 1834 as an illustration of the effects of crime within a local area.[3] Later in the decade, in 1839, evidence given before a parliamentry inquiry into crime in Ireland suggests that King's County was still regarded as very unsettled, and that it was 'next to impossible' to live in the county without being sworn into a secret society.[4] Although counties Tipperary and Limerick were the most 'consistently disturbed' counties in Ireland in the first half of the nineteenth century,[5] it is clear that, at times, King's County was seriously disturbed, and the barony of Garrycastle particularly so.

The violence which afflicted the area around Ferbane during the mid-to-late 1830s can be divided into two main categories. The first category is violence which was related to what were variously referred to as 'systems', 'combinations' or secret societies. Secret societies usually concerned themselves with issues involving land and employment. All other crimes fall into the second category – those *not* associated with any organised system of unrest. Included under this heading are crimes arising out of disputes with neighbours, drunkenness, faction fighting, violence at fairs, and crimes involving women such as rape and infanticide.

The 1830s witnessed a resurgence in agrarian secret societies.[6] Agrarian violence was most common among 'peasants who lived slightly above the margin of complete poverty, and still had something to lose'.[7] Although, by the 1830s, the peasants of King's County were certainly poor, they were not as badly off as their counterparts west of the Shannon, some of whom aroused resentment in Ferbane when they came into the area looking for work or to buy potatoes. As the local population increased, and as poverty became more ingrained in the community, secret societies attempted to appropriate responsibility for the organisation of employment and the distribution of land within the area. Details of the activities of the secret societies survive in police records dating from the 1830s.

Agrarian violence around Ferbane was carried out under a variety of names: Captain Rock, Captain Steel, Captain Starlight, Captain Terry or Terryalts, Blackfeet and Ribbonmen. Whatever name was adopted, many threatening notices referred to the 'law' of the secret societies. Labourers employed by a road contractor near Birr in February 1835 were warned not to break 'Terryalt laws' by working for less than 1s. a day. When James Crowe of Clongowney took a few acres from which the previous occupant had been evicted, shots were fired at his house, windows were broken, and the ears and tails of two horses cut. The assailants remarked that 'they had to acquaint him with the rules of the country'. Another time, 'Captain Steel' warned people against giving evidence at a case soon to come before Belmont petty sessions: 'if any person dare presume to violate my laws I will make them smell the powder of my gun'.[8] The law of a secret society was stronger than any government law. Mrs. King's nephew, Lord Oxmantown, writing in 1834, explained why this was so:

> The combination [i.e. secret society] is directly opposed to the law, and it is stronger than it, because it punishes the violations of its mandates with more severity and infinitely more certainty than the law does.[9]

Agrarian agitators around Ferbane in the 1830s were not seeking to radically change the land system as it then operated in Ireland, and the ending of landlordism was never contemplated. The one threatening letter sent to the Rev. Henry King during this period was couched mostly in respectful terms, and the writer affected concern about King's welfare. King was assured that he would not be troubled again if the writer's demand was granted. Lee states that land agitators before the Famine,

> sought to enforce a code of good conduct within the terms of the existing tenurial system. They pursued a limited, concrete, pragmatic programme.[10]

Although the 'existing tenurial system' was under severe pressure due to increasing competition for land, conflict tended to occur between competing sets of occupiers, and not between tenants and landlords. The landlords involved in the vast majority of disputes were not the local gentry landowners such as the Rev. Henry King of Ballylin, R.J.E. Mooney of Doon, or Col. L'Estrange of Moystown, but a lower layer of strong farmers and middlemen who did not hesitate, at times, to use unscrupulous methods to rid themselves of unwanted tenants. Lewis stated that two objectives of secret societies were, 'to keep the actual occupant in possession of his land . . . [and] to regulate the relation of landlord and tenant for the benefit of the latter . . .'[11] Using crude threats and frequent cruel reprisals, Captain Rock and his cohorts attempted to enforce their law among the peasantry. For example, in 1835, Captain Rock warned people around Ballycumber not to interfere with land from which a local woman had been evicted: 'we will not let our sister be broke in upon [sic] . . . any one that meddles with it after this may prepare for death and destruction.' Three men who took over ground that had lain unoccupied for three years at Kilnagarna were severely beaten by an armed gang and ordered to give up the land. At Bellair, a horse which had been used to plough land from which another occupant had been evicted was maimed.[12] People, houses, crops and animals were liable to be attacked even where evictions had not taken place, but where previous tenants had themselves given up a house or land for which they could no longer pay rent. The extent of land hunger around Ferbane in the 1830s can be measured by the fact that people were willing to risk the vengeful displeasures of Captains Rock, Steel, Terry or Starlight in their eagerness to acquire ground. Around 1830, an entire family, the Murphys of Cloghan, had been killed when their cabin was set on fire.[13]

Apart from their land-related activities, secret societies also concerned themselves with matters pertaining to employment and wages. Around Ferbane, this generally meant seeking to impose certain minimum wages, preventing the employment of strangers and, in some cases, determining who was employed by whom. Some crimes, especially those directed against the Grand Canal Company, were intended to help create employment. The high level of labour-related crime in the area reflected the lack of steady employment available locally, and the desperation of members of the community to find work – any work – however badly paid. But it was the poor themselves, and not their relatively well-off employers, who suffered most as a result of employment related crime.

Rather then forcing wages up, 'Terryalt laws' meant that several men left the employment of a road contractor carrying out repairs on the Birr-Banagher route when labourers were forbidden to work for less than a shilling a day. Patrick Lally of Clonlara was beaten up and ordered not to work for a farmer named Duffy for less than 10*d*. a day. Four members of the Cusack family were assaulted by three members of the Dolan family in a dispute over a work contract for the Grand Canal Company.[14] In a situation of gross underemployment, where labourers beat each other up competing for badly-paid work, the secret societies were fighting a loosing battle in their attempts to push up wages. In 1837, the Rev. Henry King was only mildly rebuked ('O shame, Mr. King, that it would be the talk of the country . . . ') for paying as little as 5*d*. a day.[15] The secret societies were more successful in driving strangers out of employment in the area. When Mary Rigney of Clonlyon was instructed to get rid of a servant girl by a man with a blunderbuss she complied with the order.[16]

The existence of secret societies within an area was undoubtedly a convenient cover for individuals pursuing private vendettas against their neighbours.[17] Many crimes were associated with fallings-out among neighbours. When John Lally of Bracca had a row with his neighbours a party of four armed men visited his house. They put Lally's wife on her knees and swore her 'to be a good neighbour', fired a shot in the house and broke some delph on the dresser. Threatening letters were sent to Elizabeth Connolly of Moystown and Catherine Connolly of Mullaghature in an attempt to force them out of their houses because they were disliked by their neighbours. When shots were fired at two houses in Kilcolgan the occupants could assign no reason for the attacks, 'having had no previous dispute with any of their neighbours'.[18]

Fairs were great occasions for drunkenness and faction fighting. The police often requested extra forces to go on duty at fairs around the area, and were sufficiently relieved to comment favourably on crowd scenes that passed off peacefully. Extra forces and a stipendary magistrate were requested for the Banagher fair in 1838, but despite rumours that the peasantry intended to violently resist the payment of tolls and customs, the fair passed off with 'the utmost tranquillity'.[19]

Faction fighting seems to have been a problem, off and on, in the area around Ferbane during the 1830s. Faction fights were sometimes pre-arranged, and the police could attempt to prevent them by deploying extra constables to the expected venue, and by requiring the leaders to 'enter into securities for their good behaviour', as was the case in a fight threatened for Clonony in November 1839. Women as well as men took part in fights. In March 1836, a 'very disgraceful riot' took place in Ferbane between the Malones on one side, and the Dudleys and Feigherys on the other, 'which was not only fought in the town, but in the chapel during divine service'. Faction fights were often linked to other events, for example a funeral in Shannonbridge, and the fair of Gallen, both in 1839. Not all faction leaders persisted with their lives of violence; a retired faction leader living near Doon eventually became 'helpful' to the police, and provided information which led to an execution and a transportation.[20] Drunkenness was a factor in many riots and fights, and illicit distillation was alleged to have been 'frightfully prevalent' in the area around Ferbane, facilitated by the proximity of the River Shannon and extensive tracts of bogland.[21]

The role of women as either the perpetrators or victims of crime in the Ferbane area cannot be separated from their status in the society of the time. In many ways women were no better or worse off than their male counterparts: they too received threatening letters, and were victims of unlawful ejectment, intimidation or theft. Although it is highly unlikely that women were fully involved in the activities of the secret societies, they did play a part in the general agrarian unrest of the 1830s. In two unconnected cases, women who had been evicted from their former cabins were suspected of later setting fire to them.[22] In another case, a group of 'unknown' women in Lumcloon prevented six cattle from being seized for rent. They 'were encouraged by several men standing by, but who did not themselves rescue the cattle or offer any violence'.[23] The women were able to take advantage of their anonymity to the officials concerned, and were perhaps less likely to be harshly treated by the law. The three officials might have been prepared for violence from the male bystanders, but were reluctant to provoke a fracas with a band of women. The case was later resolved at Belmont petty sessions.

If women were free to play a part in the agrarian conflicts of the time, they were certainly not free in other regards. Certain crimes reflect how women were the main victims of inflexible moral and social codes. Young people (male or female) were not free to choose their own marriage partners, and it is likely that a number of crimes committed in the Ferbane area during this period were a result of frustration with the usual marriage practices. The attempted kidnapping of Catherine Rigney from her sister's house at Galros failed in February 1838. The attackers, it was suspected, had hoped to carry her off 'for some young man'. It is possible that this incident might have ended in nothing more sinister than marriage. Another time, a young woman from Lumcloon made an allegation of rape against a neighbour, but the police believed the object of the complainant was 'to induce him to marry her'.[24]

During the late 1830s, the bodies of three infants were found in the area around Ferbane. One mother was the wife of a soldier on foreign service, and the baby was found to have died of natural causes. The mother of an infant who died of neglect was found to have 'feloniously concealed' the birth and secretly interred the body, and was committed to jail for trial at the next assizes. In a third case, the body of a male infant who had been strangled was found in a stream at Killourney. A 'wanted' poster was drawn up, and a large reward of £20 offered for information leading to the arrest of the killer.[25] Disapproval of single mothers was obviously so strong that some women attempted to obliterate the evidence.

Several incidents of rape were reported in the Ferbane area in the late 1830s. In the six years between 1835 and 1840, twenty-eight charges of rape were recorded for the whole of King's County, but not one of these charges resulted in conviction.[26] The apparent impossibility of successfully prosecuting a case of rape meant that some women felt justified in taking the law into their own hands. In 1838, the turf stack of a man in Lemonaghan was set on fire by a girl who had failed in an attempt to bring a charge of rape against him at Doon petty sessions.[27]

Gloomy contemporary views held that in a crime blighted barony such as Garrycastle, 'terror reigns everywhere' and 'evil . . . spreads to all'.[28] It is doubtful, however, whether all of the people living around Ferbane felt that they were living through a crisis. The contradictory answers given in response to a question on law-and-order in the Poor Inquiry in 1836 – ranging from 'much disturbed' to 'in general peaceable' – show that attitudes to crime varied hugely even within the same parish.[29]

Among the gentry classes it was probably a matter of pride not to be seen to give in to the demands of secret societies. The Rev. Henry King reported the threatening letter he received in 1837 to the police, but ignored the instruction that he dismiss his land steward. Mr. Robert Lauder, J.P., a close friend of the King family, resident in the same parish, and the victim of several attacks against his property, refused to alter his estate management style to suit the 'law' of the secret societies. In July 1838, a school house, the property of Lauder, was burned down after the school master was given notices to quit. A year later, an unoccupied house which had been given up by a tenant who could no longer pay rent was also burned down. When Lauder raised the rents of his tenants in Lusmagh (near Banagher), the shapes of a grave and a gun were carved into a sheep-walk he owned. Despite this, within a few months, Lauder had thirty-seven sheep and two cows impounded at Aghaboy when tenants around Ferbane fell behind in their rents.[30] (The animals were subsequently stolen from the pound.)

The gentry classes were rarely affected by the activities of secret societies in the area around Ferbane. Random or unaccountable crimes against the gentry were few in number. Mr. John Bernard of Ferbane could give no reason why an ear should have been cut off his horse. Four sheep belonging to Mr. James Armstrong of Castle Iver (in Gallen) were 'plucked in a most cruel manner' for no apparent reason.[31] Even if the sole purpose of such crimes was to strike terror into the hearts of the upper classes, it was not true that members of the local gentry fortified their houses and only went abroad armed.[32] Mrs. King's diary for 1838 shows that the Kings felt completely at ease in their surroundings, and spent a lot of their time walking, riding and driving around the local area. The only outrage mentioned by Mrs. King – the murder of Lord Norbury – did not happen locally, and was so exceptional that she wrote it into her diary even though it happened in 1839:

> On new year's day – 1839 – Lord Norbury was shot near his house at Durrow Abbey at about 4 o'clock in the afternoon & died of his wound on Thursday the 3rd.[33]

It was undoubtedly much easier, and probably more successful for agrarian societies to 'confine their attacks to members of the lower classes'.[34] In all categories of crime affecting the Ferbane area during the 1830s, the victims were overwhelmingly drawn from among the ranks of the poor.

The ordinary forces of law-and-order could not cope with the level of crime around Ferbane, nor were they expected to. The Belmont magistrates, in 1834, hoped that by having Garrycastle declared as in a state of 'disturbance and insubordination', they could circumvent the usual impediments to successful prosecutions such as intimidation of witnesses and perjury.[35] Police reports for the area around Ferbane show how intimidation of both victims and witnesses of violence, and general antipathy towards the police meant that, to a considerable extent, the secret societies could break the law with impunity.

Monthly returns of the numbers of outrages in an area were based on reports of crimes that were 'known to the police'.[36] It is obvious that many crimes in the Ferbane area only came to police attention by chance, and it follows that many more must have gone unreported. An outrage committed on the canal at Gillen was 'never mentioned or reported . . . to any individual of the constabulary force, although the police were, and are, on the banks of the canal every evening'. Attacks on cabins in Noggis and Lumcloon went unreported as the inhabitants were afraid that if it was known that they had been in touch with the police they would be burned in their cabins. Two brothers who were assaulted in Banagher for having given evidence in a case of sheep stealing two years previously failed to report the incident to the police on the spurious grounds that they 'did not know where the barrack was'.[37] They had learned their lesson.

Another set of crimes concerns those in which the victims or witnesses refused to give evidence about the identity of their attackers, or even to admit that an offence had taken place. The relatives of a young man who died after an altercation in Corcoran's public house at Doon tried to persuade the police that the death 'was not caused by any violence'. A man in Lemonaghan was put on his knees and had priming burned over his head in a dispute about a house, but the police officer writing the report stated, 'I have very little hope of his telling who they were, even if he knows them'. A woman who had been robbed in Cloghan evaded coming forward to prosecute when a number of men were brought to trial. They were discharged.[38]

According to their own reports, the police were active and flexible in their efforts to combat crime in the area around Ferbane. They patrolled by night and day, and sent extra forces to deal with potential trouble-spots such as fairs, sales of impounded animals, emigrant embarkation points along the canal, or the sites of prospective faction fights. In 1837 and 1838, offers of rewards by the lord lieutenant for the discovery of the perpetrators of murders and other outrages went unclaimed for all of King's County.[39] At times, constables were assigned to protect individual households which were under threat of attack. A Clonony man who had defended his house against attack was given a gun (which was later stolen from him) for his own protection.[40]

The sixty or so policemen who looked after the barony of Garrycastle were an isolated group in the community around Ferbane. The gentry had little or nothing to do with them – Mrs. King not once referred to the police in her diary of 1838 – and they were regarded with distrust by a large portion of the population. Many peasants saw little point in co-operating with a force which had 'no power to protect' them.[41] Policemen were occasionally attacked, and a threatening letter warned the public against doing business with a retired policeman, John Saunders, who had set up a shop at Mullaghature.[42]

Police stations were established in all the main centres of population around Ferbane; Ferbane itself, Cloghan, Ballycumber, Shannonbridge, Shannon Harbour and Clonfinlough. Despite the presence of policemen within the community, it was recognised that the peasantry could not be restrained by any means of patrolling:

> Every police station is closely watched; the police cannot stir that it is not instantly known. When on duty, even on the darkest night, their course is easily discernible from the barking of dogs, as almost every cottage is provided with one.[43]

Lord Oxmantown regarded the magistrates of King's County as 'numerous and efficient . . . zealous and upright',[44] although of the five magistrates listed for Belmont in 1835, one had resigned, another was incapacitated due to 'age and infirmity', and a third was sojourning in Germany.[45] The magistrates could examine victims and witnesses of crimes under oath, but complained that unwilling witnesses resorted to the 'grossest perjury' in order to procure acquittals. Bonfires were lit on every hill to celebrate the failure of the Tullamore assizes in March 1834.[46]

The number of convictions for crimes in King's County failed to match a substantial rise in the number of committals to the county's jails during the 1830s. The governor of Tullamore jail reported that committals to the jails of Tullamore and Philipstown rose from 699 in 1835, to 1,044 in 1838, a rise of 33 per cent.[47] During the same period the number of convictions at Tullamore (alone) rose from only forty-six to fifty-four, a rise of 15 per cent, less than half the rate of increase in the number of committals.[48] Chief Constable Henderson, who was in charge of the Ferbane district in the mid-1830s, reported that 'lawless characters' were still afloat in the area, 'notwithstanding the severe examples that have been made at several assizes of like characters from this district'.[49] The coming together of the magistrates in Belmont in 1834 to set down formal resolutions about the state of King's County as regards crime and outrage, proves that the local gentry were capable of forming themselves into a cohesive group in order to secure a particular objective; in this case, the official declaration that the barony of Garrycastle was in a state of 'disturbance and subordination'. However, even at this moment of perceived crisis, the magistrates' aims were limited. They merely hoped to restrain lawlessness 'within moderate bounds', and they were aware that any increase in the

numbers of police or military in the area, and the granting of extra powers to
them, would be more symbolic than effectual: 'the only useful result of it
would be to show that the disturbances in that barony had not altogether
escaped the notice of government.'[50]

It could be argued that by self-consciously confining themselves to cos-
metic gestures, the local figures of authority were simply being realistic. They
were admitting, in effect, that there was little or nothing that they could do to
reduce the level of crime in the area. Most of them were personally unaffected
by crime, and although they sympathised with the 'industrious peasantry' who
were allegedly living in a state of 'perpetual anxiety',[51] very little was done to
help them during the rest of the 1830s.

Lewis, in his account of local disturbances in Ireland, explained that many
of the causes of rural crime were linked to poverty, and he urged that there
should be 'legal provision' for the poor. The workhouse system, established in
Ireland during the late 1830s, was designed to cater only for the destitute poor,
but the destitute poor were not regarded, even in the 1830s, as the main insti-
gators of unrest in rural Ireland: 'disturbances . . . appear to prevail more where
the peasantry are bold and robust, and one degree removed above the lowest
poverty.'[52] It is unlikely, therefore, that the building of a workhouse in Birr
brought crime in the area around Ferbane to an end.

Social Affairs

As resident landowners on a profitably run estate of several thousand acres, and as proprietors of the town of Ferbane, the Kings enjoyed high social and economic status within the local area, and could have exerted a powerful influence on public affairs in the community around Ferbane, and particularly over the lives of the 1,500 or so people who resided on their property in the late 1830s. Irish landlords before the Famine,

> ... represented the peak of the Irish social pyramid. In addition to owning land they controlled parliamentary seats and furnished members of parliament; they also dominated local government and the administration of law and order.[1]

Landlord families closely related to the Kings, such as the earls of Rosse, or Mrs. King's own family, the Lloyds of Gloster (near Birr), fell into this category, as did several of their landowning neighbours in the Ferbane area. Fellow landlords in Garrycastle served at various times as justices of the peace, high sheriff, lord lieutenant and vice-lieutenant of King's County, as poor law guardians and as parliamentary candidates and members of parliament. The Rev. Henry King never sought or held any of these offices. It seems that King precluded himself from public life because he was in holy orders. In 1827, he had felt it necessary to seek legal advice as to whether he could hold the office of church warden.[2] Unlike other local landowners, he did not submit evidence to important parliamentary investigations of the time such as the Poor Inquiry, 1836, or the Devon Commission, 1845. It is possible that he lent his support and influence to certain public figures, but the only written evidence relates to his holdings in County Leitrim. A letter from Lord Leitrim requested a 'repetition' of his support for Lord Leitrim's son in a forthcoming general election.[3]

The population of King's County stood at 144,225 in 1831, yet there were a mere 1,694 registered electors in the county in 1836.[4] Despite the fact that only slightly over 1 per cent of the population could vote, there was widespread public interest in elections, even among those not included in the franchise. People from both ends of the social scale in the Ferbane area played active parts in the 1837 general election. Local landowners proposed opposing candidates for election, and a local man, Peter Kelly of Clonfinlough, was accused of being the leader of a mob which 'grievously assaulted James Grant Esq. in the town of Cloghan on 7 August 1837, during the contested election'.[5] Col. L'Estrange of Moystown was involved in attempts to establish a Conservative Association in King's County, 'for the purpose of rescuing the King's County from the grasp of the enemies of the Established Church and the throne' during the 1830s.[6] The *Dublin Evening Post* criticised Lord Oxmantown and Col. Lloyd (Mrs. King's nephew and brother, respectively) for subscribing to Tory funds even though they both held government offices in the county.[7]

Sectarian divisions were a badge of political loyalty to the Conservatives of King's County in the late 1830s. This period has been identified as a time of heightened sectarian feelings in Ireland generally.[8] The struggle for Catholic emancipation, the tithe war, and the establishment of proselytising schools and evangelical missionary movements all contributed to bitterness between Catholics and Protestants at national and local levels. Outbreaks of violence associated with the tithe war, sectarianism in the administration of charity, and personal bigotry can be identified in records relating to the Ferbane area, although such examples probably tend to distort unreported normal behaviour in the local population. A proselytising school and an evangelical 'Home Mission' movement existed in Ferbane during the late 1830s.

The Catholic population around Ferbane vastly outnumbered the non-Catholic population. In 1834, in the parish of Wheery (King's parish), there were 3,293 Catholics, 275 members of the Church of Ireland, no Presbyterians, and seventeen other Dissenters.[9] This meant that 91·85 per cent of the population was Catholic, and 7·67 per cent Church of Ireland.

Despite the Kings' commitment to evangelical causes, relations between the Rev. Henry King and the local Catholic population were apparently cordial. A new chapel (a Roman Catholic church) was built in Ferbane during the early 1830s on land provided by King who gave the parish priest, Fr. Edward Keogh, a perpetual lease on half an acre of ground at Kilmore for 2s. 6d. per annum. A letter from Fr. Keogh also thanked King for a 'kind, polite & liberal communication' which King had sent in response to an earlier letter requesting a subscription towards the new church, and gratefully acknowledged the 'obligation . . . conferred on the people of this parish as well as myself' by King's generosity.[10]

Several examples of sectarian ill-will can be identified in the outrage reports of the late 1830s. During a raid on the Cunningham household in Fadden, one of the attackers called Mrs. Cunningham an 'Orange bitch'. Sectarian anger was easily provoked. A traveller passing through Ferbane in 1839 paid a fiddler a few pence to play a Protestant song, 'on which account some of the townspeople assembled at the time got irritated'. The police were directed to escort the traveller out of town, but when they left him at Corr

Hill, two miles away, he was assaulted.[11] Other crimes were linked to the tithe war. They were generally directed against those who had paid their tithes, not against those who collected or received them. A dog belonging to William Lowe of Lemonaghan, a yeoman who had paid his tithes, was shot. Shots were fired at a house in Bracca, and a threatening notice was delivered, saying, 'Denis Kyran, that if you or John Ryan pay any tithe . . . I will shoot both of you as dead as Norbury'.[12] The Catholic clergy in the Ferbane area supported the maintenance of law and order, and encouraged their parishioners to report crimes to the police. A man who had been severely beaten in Cloghan would not have reported the assault only he was advised to do so by his priest. On at least two occasions in the late 1830s, the parish priest of Ferbane acted as a go-between in the surrender of arms to the local constabulary.[13]

As a member of the parish vestry, the Rev. Henry King was influential in local Church of Ireland affairs, but on only one occasion during 1838, on Easter Sunday, did he assist in the conduct of divine service. He oversaw the renovation of the parish church in 1838, and he was consulted about the allocation of pews.[14] Many entries in Mrs. King's diary of 1838 concern church matters, and on no less than seventeen occasions she makes reference to Home Missions.

The Established Church Home Mission, founded in 1828, was an evangelical missionary movement which aimed to revive the Church by proselytising among Roman Catholics.[15] Mrs. King would have approved of this aim as she believed that 'the spirit of popery' in Ireland was 'a bar to improvement in any way'.[16] A laudatory account of the Home Mission movement as it operated near Banagher (less than eight miles away) was written by a contemporary travel writer:

> A neat room has been fitted up for worship in which I heard an excellent sermon from the missionary . . . [Home Missions have brought] a considerable increase of religious feeling . . . there are now ten missionary circuits, travelled by above 100 zealous ministers of the Church of Ireland . . . The missionaries do not at present reach the Roman Catholics or the great landholders, their work lying chiefly among the smaller gentry and the middle class of Protestants.[17]

Even though the number of people attending Home Missions in the Ferbane area was not large – around thirty-six people on one occasion in October 1838 – the missionary movement probably provided a welcome sense of renewed fervour, strength and unity to at least some of the Protestant population around Ferbane.

The Kings also displayed their religious zeal by acting as patrons to a school set up in the late in the late 1830s under the aegis of the London Hibernian

Society. This proselytising body aimed to civilise the people of Ireland through a 'reduction of popery'. In order to erect and furnish suitable school houses, and to allow adequate salaries to the teachers, the London Hibernian Society relied on financial support from 'powerful local patrons'.[18] Although there were London Hibernian schools in Lemonaghan and Clonmacnoise in 1834, there was none at that time in Ferbane.[19] In her diary of 1838, Mrs. King refered more than once to the 'new' school house, and also called it 'our' school house. She and her husband took an active interest in the school, visiting it several times during the year. Their three daughters, (then aged fourteen, twelve and eleven years) spent time teaching the children, although this ended when the King parents became concerned that their daughters' health was suffering through contact with the school children who numbered about fifty-six in October 1838. The Kings attended examinations by the inspector of the London Hibernian Society, and 'felt much gratified' on these occasions.[20]

The establishment of a London Hibernian School in Ferbane in the mid-to-late 1830s directly contradicted the ideals of the recently inaugurated national school system in Ireland, which was intended to promote a non-denominational system of education. The Kings obviously opposed the national system which had been condemned by the Anglican bishop of Meath (in which diocese Ferbane lay), and was regarded as 'pernicious' by midland conservatives.[21] In March 1832, an application for aid for a national school in Cloghan, signed by eleven Protestants and eighteen Catholics, was made to the new Board of Commissioners for National Education, but no application was received from Ferbane until nearly twenty years later, in 1851, by which time the national system was effectively denominational.[22]

Although by the late 1830s there were only four official national schools in the area (Cloghan male, Cloghan female, Shannon Harbour and High Street),[23] the Ordnance Survey name books and Lewis' *Topographical dictionary* record the existence of other schools in the locality, and a widespread interest in education:

> Though illiterate, they [i.e. the peasants of King's County] are very anxious to have their children instructed, as is evident from the number of small schools in all parts.[24]

In 1835, a parliamentary report identified a total of nineteen schools, only two of which were official national schools, in the parishes of Wheery, Gallen and Tisaran.[25] Of the schools for which pupil numbers are given, most had between thirty-five and seventy children on their rolls at the time of inspection. The national schools in Cloghan and High Street had ninety-five and 153 students respectively. In all but two schools the source of support was listed as 'payment

by children', although this was occasionally supplemented by the provision of
a house and garden by a local landowner.

Most schools were described as 'hedge schools', and had precarious existences.
Many produced no list of pupils, and those which did generally reported a
lower average daily attendance than the number of children given on their
lists. No school had been in existence for longer than two and a half years and
teachers' salaries were low. Payments by children were as low as 1*d*. per week
in some schools, perhaps reflecting poverty in the area around Ferbane in the
mid-1830s. Another indication of poverty was that despite the reported
anxiety for education among the illiterate peasantry of King's County, only a
minority of children in the Ferbane area were enrolled in any school in 1835.
Although the total population of the three parishes rose from 9,563 in 1831
to 11,716 in 1841, the school-going population amounted to only 1,062 in
1835. Boys were almost twice as likely as girls to receive an education; 65·35
per cent of the school population was male, with only 34·65 per cent female.

The gender imbalance within the schooling system was also reflected in
literacy levels among the local population. The 1841 census sought information
on the literacy of all persons aged five years and upwards.[26] Literacy among
males was consistently higher than literacy among females, both in the town
of Ferbane and in the surrounding rural area. Overall, 37·51 per cent of males
claimed to be fully literate whereas the corresponding figure for females was
only 18·70 per cent. It is noticeable that town dwellers had significantly higher
literacy levels than those who lived in the surrounding rural area. Only 27·19
per cent of rural dwellers described themselves as fully literate, but in Ferbane
town, 46·60 per cent of the population was literate. It thus seems that males
living in the town had gained most from the haphazard educational system
that operated around the Ferbane area in the first half of the nineteenth
century, with 52·70 per cent of town males able to read and write. The most
deprived, in terms of education, were rural females, only 17·70 per cent of
whom were described as fully literate in 1841. Higher literacy rates in the
town may have reflected the higher proportion of people involved in trade in
the town area, although literacy was not a prerequisite for those who wished
to be employed in trade. John Saunders, who had been discharged from the
police force for not knowing how to write, set himself up as a shop-keeper
with the compensation money granted him by the government for his 'long
and faithful services'.[27]

The Irish language was not used around Ferbane by the late 1830s. It was
regarded as the mark of a stranger: 'They speak English everywhere [in King's
County]; if a person is heard speaking Irish, they invariably call him a
Connaughtman'.[28] Documentary records from among the ranks of the poor
are few, and are mainly confined to the threatening letter genre. All such letters
and notices are in English and most display anomalies in spelling, grammar
and punctuation.

The programmes of instruction available to the pupils of the various hedge schools and parish schools around Ferbane were all fairly similar.[29] Reading, writing and arithmetic were offered in most schools, with one school in Cloghan also offering book-keeping and mensuration. A few schools limited themselves to spelling and reading. Sectarian divisions in education were apparent, with some schools offering 'scriptural instruction' and others offering 'Roman Catholic catechism'. A number of schools also taught needlework. One establishment at Moystown offered 'reading, writing and needlework' to fifteen or twenty female students. The teacher, Mrs. Horne, derived her income from the produce of the children's work. There is no way of knowing whether her pupils' reading and writing skills matched their sewing skills.

The Rev. Henry King and his wife meanwhile ensured that their own children received a much broader education at home. In her diary of 1838, Mrs. King mentioned that John (who was then around sixteen years of age) said his lessons to a local clergyman, 'Mr. T.', who was a frequent visitor at Ballylin. John King later read law at Trinity College, Dublin. The Kings' three daughters, Harriet, Jane and Mary, (born in 1824, 1826 and 1827 respectively) were under the care of a 'Miss C.' who lived with the family. A 'commonplace' book kept by Harriet King in the late 1830s contains notes on Italian grammar and German literature, and Mrs. King referred to a Chinese dictionary in her diary of 1838.[30] The King girls probably studied music as there were at least two pianos in the house, and it is also likely that they studied art. The King parents encouraged their daughters' interests and talents. Mary King's early interest in natural history was fostered from the age of seven with gifts of books on the subject. Later, on the advice of the astronomer Sir James South, her father bought a microscope for Mary's use, which at the time of its arrival in Ballylin in 1845, was considered to have been the finest microscope in Ireland. Under her married name, Mary King published three books on natural history and many scientific papers.[31]

The Kings could provide their children with an excellent education, but they could not protect them against illness. During 1838, all four children and Mrs. King herself were afflicted with whooping cough. Several entries in Mrs. King's diary show great anxiety about her children's health. The Rev. Henry King was confined to his room for many days with gout, and was unable at times to walk or ride. Also during 1838, he suffered from rheumatism, and he dislocated his shoulder in a fall from a horse. Mrs. King seems frequently to have had colds or headaches. The Kings could afford to summon medical help whenever they liked. Dr. Fry, who lived in Ferbane, would come at any time, and sometimes stayed overnight if members of the family were particularly unwell. In February 1838, the coachman was dispatched to bring a Dr. Kelly and a Dr. Bewley to see Mary, whose condition was considered alarming. When her children recovered from their various bouts of illness Mrs. King expressed thanks to God rather than to the doctors, 'Mary better, thank God!'[32]

Although money was no object to the Kings and their wealthy neighbours, it is clear from Mrs. King's diary that even the best medical care available in the late 1830s was, at times, confusing and unreliable. Their friend and neighbour, Mr. Daly of Castledaly, became unwell during 1838, and consulted physicians in Dublin about his illness. Mrs. King's comments on Mr. Daly's condition varied wildly from day to day. A 'very unfavourable account' of Mr. Daly was followed a few days later by an 'unexpectedly good account'. Subsequently, Mrs. King gloomily concluded that she did not know what to think of Mr. Daly's condition, 'the accounts are so variable and contradictory'. Mr. Daly died some three months later. Miss Mooney of Doon, a member of another prominent local landlord family, died of typhus in November 1838.[33]

It is impossible to ascertain general death rates or the causes of death among the population at large. Outbreaks of 'fever' during the 1830s are mentioned in some sources, but it is unlikely that Andy Moore, a tenant on King's estate, or Anne Lynch of Bracca, were the only local fatalities during this period.[34] There was a fever hospital in Birr and dispensaries in Ferbane, Banagher and Clara, 'supported equally by private contributions and grand jury present-ments'.[35] During the 1830s, Mr. Robert Lauder of Moyclare, a friend of the Kings, acted as treasurer to the dispensary in Ferbane, to which the grand jury granted the sum of £16. 19s. in 1838.[36] The Ferbane dispensary served a population of at least 9,000 people in the surrounding area.

Members of the gentry class, who had servants to look after all their requirements, and poor people who could find no work probably had exten-sive free time on their hands. Mrs. King's diary gives details of how the King family and their gentry neighbours occupied their leisure time. Gardening was Mrs. King's favourite pastime, and occupied a significant amount of her time throughout the year. She was regarded as an expert gardener by neighbouring gentry folk who consulted her on the layout of their gardens. Indoors, Mrs. King did needlework, read books, and had pianos at her disposal. In December 1838, a cabinet was ordered from Dublin into which she placed 'little curiosi-ties'. The menfolk went out fox hunting, and also shot grouse and partridges etc. During 1838 the King family, accompanied by a number of servants, went on a six-week tour of England and Wales.[37]

Information about pastimes among the poor is available indirectly from official and police records, and not from the poor themselves. Some local landowners thought that the poor were naturally 'idle' and that they wasted their lives on 'whiskey, politics and card-playing'.[38] The high number of public houses in the Ferbane area, and references to drunkenness at fairs and other public occasions, would seen to indicate that heavy drinking was widespread. Disturbances at public entertainments sometimes warranted police intervention, and so it is possible to learn what kind of diversions were available, from time to time, to the people living around Ferbane in the 1830s. A company of actors toured the area in 1838, and erected a booth in which to put on their show. A thirteen year old girl was injured when a stone was thrown into the crowd. Musicians, whether local or not it is impossible to say, played and sang on the street in Ferbane. The local police force expressed concern about the establishment of a 'Shooting Gallery' in Banagher, 'where numbers of persons attended to practise firing at a mark for the small charge of one penny per shot'.[39] It is likely that local people enjoyed other pastimes such as singing, dancing, story-telling and games of various types, but specific references to any such activities are not to be found.

The conduct of public and social affairs in Ferbane during the 1830s – whether in the area of education, health, politics, religion or recreation – highlights the division that existed within local society between those who had money and those who had not. Wealth, or the lack of it was the key dividing line. It often coincided with an individual's religious allegiance and sometimes determined political loyalties. Wealth always determined the quality of health or educational services to which an individual had access. Even where both rich and poor may have shared identical interests, for example in whiskey, politics and cardplaying, they followed these pursuits in strictly separate circumstances.

Conclusion

The most striking feature of the community which inhabited the area around Ferbane during the late 1830s is the enormous difference between the lives of the rich and poor members of local society. Although they shared the same landscape, and were linked by strong bonds such as the landlord-tenant or employer-worker relationships, records for the area around Ferbane show that there were few direct contacts between them. The opening of the threatening letter sent to the Rev. Henry King in 1837 ('I cannot get over writing to your honour . . .') shows how unusual it was for a member of the underclass to initiate direct contact with a man of King's status. Prolonged wet weather rained down on rich and poor alike during the summer of 1838, but they were not affected in the same way. Whereas Mrs. King expressed sadness about her withered roses and broken dahlias, poor people in the area were sickened by their sodden potatoes.

The wealthy members of local society accounted for only a tiny proportion of the population, but they literally owned the landscape around Ferbane and reserved significant portions of it for their personal use. The Kings of Ballylin were part of a local group of resident landlords who formed an élite layer in society around Ferbane. These minor gentry figures, who owned estates of several thousand acres each, were themselves dwarfed by major landowners such as the earls of Rosse (Birr) and Charleville (Tullamore), who controlled tens of thousands of acres in King's County. Around Ferbane, the Kings and their friends constituted a self-contained social network who lived quite contentedly and utterly separately from the poverty-stricken, potato-eating, predominantly Catholic, peasantry around them.

It would be erroneous, however, to give the impression that Ferbane was a society composed purely of two extremes. There existed an intermediary layer comprising roughly one-quarter of the local population. These were the people who lived in the houses categorised as second class in the 1841 census, and among whom would have been innkeepers, shopkeepers and strong farmers from the locality. It is likely that a high proportion of these people were literate, yet records relating to them do not survive. The amount of information concerning this middle layer of local society contained in official records such as parliamentary papers and outrage reports, or in private records such as those associated with the King estate, is negligible. It is regrettable that the lives of this relatively prosperous section of the local population are so poorly reflected in the available records.

The town of Ferbane and the rural area around it (the parishes of Wheery, Gallen and Tisaran) together experienced a population growth of over 22 per cent in the decade between 1831 and 1841. A substantial portion of the local landscape was covered by bog, there was no significant industry and little tradition of emigration. The Ferbane area was thus unable to absorb the population increase comfortably, and local inhabitants resorted increasingly to subdivision and monoculture despite the disapproval of local landowners. The declining living standards of a large portion of the local population were described by the parish priest of Ferbane in 1836 when he stated that the farming classes as well as the labouring poor had 'fallen into wretchedness'. By the late 1830s the poor members of the community around Ferbane were close to breaking point. Bad weather, for example in 1830 and 1838, reduced many families almost to starvation. People regarded as strangers could no longer be tolerated and were ruthlessly driven out. In one incident, family members robbed a dying woman of her store of potatoes. The past was idealised as a lost era of 'superfluous hospitality', but the future was menacing. In 1836, one commentator in King's County predicted that 'a heap of misery is likely to be generated'.

Nevertheless, the Ferbane area as a whole was relatively prosperous when compared to some other parts of Ireland. Connaught labourers were still attracted to the Ferbane area in the late 1830s despite local hostility to them. The financial success of the Ballylin Estate was underpinned by a solid block of prosperous tenant farmers who must have paid their rents with pleasing regularity. The 1830s were years of growing prosperity for the Rev. Henry King, whose investments in government stock rose by 48 per cent during the 1830s as compared to the 1820s. According to Fr. O'Farrell, the parish priest of Ferbane, high rents contributed to the wretched state of the local peasantry. The threatening letter sent to King in 1837 reproached King for paying low wages but not for charging high rents. The most expensive rents around Ferbane were not charged by landlords such as King, but by tenant-farmer middlemen who expected under-employed, poorly-paid labourers to give the equivalent of their entire annual income for an acre or less of potato ground.

One of the aims of this study was to investigate how different groups of people attempted to influence each other. In theory, the Rev. Henry King could have wielded widespread influence within the community around Ferbane, but apart from the fact that he owned the land on which a significant portion of local people lived, his impact was minimal. Unlike other landowners in the locality, he played no part in the political or public life of the area; he did nothing to develop the town of Ferbane or to encourage local industry; he gave no instructions on land use, and turned a blind eye to subdivision and monoculture. He dispensed a certain amount of charity and responded favourably to occasional requests for aid from local Catholic clergymen. As a resident landowner who regularly travelled around the local countryside, King was a constant but relatively inert presence in the lives of local people. Other local landlords, such as Mooney and Mullock, who attempted to intervene directly in the lives of their tenants felt that their efforts were futile as the poor ignored their advice. The poor, lacking the usual instruments of influence such as property, wealth or even the franchise, resorted at times to crime in their attempts to secure certain minimum standards in matters relating to land tenure and employment. The fact that crime rates remained high and wage levels low shows that crime, as a method of persuasion, was a failure. Such crimes served as a form of protest, and may have signified despair, but they also made the difficult lives of the poor more miserable.

This study has attempted to portray the circumstances that affected the lives of the people who inhabited the area around Ferbane in the late 1830s. Many of these circumstances were, to a lesser or greater extent, common to other parts of Ireland. The observation that a 'heap of misery' was likely to befall the labouring poor of King's County was true for all of Ireland. However, there was a particular combination of circumstances existing in Ferbane during the 1830s which distinguished the area from all other parts of Ireland. Around Ferbane these particular circumstances included the town's geographical location amidst extensive bogland in western Leinster, the Rev. Henry King's proprietorship over the town and several thousand acres in the area, and the relatively high incidence of crime within the barony of Garrycastle. The distinctive features of the history of a local community enrich our understanding of that area and of Ireland as a whole. The study of local history in Ireland exposes the similarities and differences that exist between and within all parts of Ireland, and deserves further exploration. As Patrick Kavanagh said, 'Parochialism is universal; it deals with the fundamentals'.[1]

Appendix

Threatening letter sent to Rev. Henry King, 11 July 1837.

Reverend Sir,

I cannot get over writing to your honour about that Nugent, your steward, that caused your men to leave you on account of terrorising over them to go to fairing country. I tell you that he is robbing you completely. Every information I am told he is building a house in Ferbane and taking ground all by the strength of your money. He is worse than ever Barr was at Col. L'Estrange's. He says he gets so many bills from his son in America. If he was coining he could not send him so much, and he giving so much money to his sons-in-law that made them rich shop-keepers. He is lodging money in bank. I am informed that he is surveying bog upon industrious people that put their dung upon dust away under the bog, and means to bring them under rent for it. I tell you, Reverend Sir, that if you did not discharge him I will give him the contents of a few shots that will ease him at a short time. Your hire is the smallest hire that is going in the country. Every gentleman gives that is in or about the neighbourhood gives 6½*d*. one half year and 8*d*. the other half year. Also I am told that there is some young boys working at 5*d*. a day that is able to do a man's work. O Shame, Mr. King, that it would be the talk of the country. I hope, Revd. Sir, that you will part that preaching villain. I do not wish to put a start or a fright in Mrs. King, as I hear she is good and charitable to the poor about her. Revd. Sir, if you do not part him I will meet you between Cloghan and Parsonstown when you are not thinking of yourself.

I am giving you timely notice to quit Ballylin, so sure as I am writing this so I swear by it, that you will get the contents of some weighty lead through your swaddling head. I will not trouble you, Revd. Sir, any more when you part that robber.

NB Another thing I forgot, the next steward you hire let him and your men keep a tally, and then every man will know what days he works. They do not know what days they have no more than the beast that is in the field. So I desire no roll call ever again from any other steward that will be hired. That villain says that every market day that he has to borrow money from Mr. Pilkington to give to those that wants to buy potatoes in the market. He makes out that you give him no money for that purpose. He is reporting you well.

Notes

ABBREVIATIONS

H.C.	House of Commons
I.H.S.	*Irish Historical Studies*
N.L.I.	National Library of Ireland
O.P.K.C.	Outrage Papers, King's County
O.S.	Ordnance Survey

The Outrage Papers are referred to according to the date of the relevant report.

INTRODUCTION

1 O.S. *Field name books, King's County*, vol. II, pp 766–80; *The census of Ireland for the year 1851*, [1550], H.C. 1852–3, xci, 429, p. 139.
2 Alan Rogers, *Approaches to local history*, (London, 1977), p. 126.
3 H.P.R. Finberg, 'Local history' in H.P.R. Finberg (ed.), *Approaches to history*, (London, 1962), pp 116–7.
4 R. Gillespie and G. Moran, 'Writing local history' in R. Gillespie, G. Moran, (eds.), *A various country, essays in Mayo history 1500–1800*, (Westport, 1987), p. 16.
5 O.S., King's County sheets 1–47, (1833–44); *Field name books, King's County*, vols. I & II, (1838); *Ordnance Survey Letters*, (1839); Samuel Lewis, *A topographical dictionary of Ireland*, (3 vols., London, 1837).
6 *Return of the population of the several counties in Ireland, as enumerated in 1831*, H.C. 1833, (254), xxxix, 1; *Report of the commissioners appointed to take the census of Ireland for the year 1841*, [504], H.C. 1843, xxiv, 1.
7 *Poor inquiry (Ireland), Appendix (D)*, [36], H.C. 1836, xxxi, 1; *Appendix (E)*, [37], H.C. 1836, xxxii, 1; *Appendix (F)*, [38], H.C. 1836, xxxiii, 1.
8 *Copies of the several documents. . . on which the baronies of Ballyboy, Ballybrit, Eglish and Garrycastle in the King's County were declared to be in a state of disturbance and insubordination*, H.C. 1834, (241), xlvii, 431.
9 National Archives, O.P.K.C. This series of reports begins in 1835.
10 Offaly County Library, Grand Jury Presentment Books, 1830–62, and Minute Books of the Board of Guardians (Parsonstown), June 1839– January 1900.
11 N.L.I., King Collection, P.C. 308–12.
12 N.L.I., Ms. 3551, Diary of Mrs. King, 1838; Ms. 3521, Servants' wages account book of the Rev. Henry King.
13 As in note 4, p. 12.
14 Henry D. Inglis, *A journey throughout Ireland, 1834*, (2 vols., London, 1835), i, p. 334.
15 H.P.R. Finberg, *The local historian and his theme*, (Leicester, 1954), pp 8–9; Margaret Spufford, *Contrasting communities, English villagers in the sixteenth and seventeenth centuries*, (Cambridge, 1974), p. xix.
16 H.P.R. Finberg, *The local historian and his theme*, (Leicester, 1954), p. 5.
17 Finberg, 'Local history', p. 37.
18 Raymond Gillespie, 'A question of survival: the O'Farrells and Longford in the seventeenth century' in R. Gillespie, G. Moran, (eds.), *Longford: essays in county history*, (Dublin, 1990), p. 26.

LOCAL LANDSCAPE AND COMMUNITY

1 E. Estyn Evans, *The personality of Ireland*, (new ed., Dublin, 1992), p. 9.
2 Samuel Lewis, *Topographical dictionary of Ireland*, (3 vols London, 1837), and O.S., *Field name books, King's County*, (1837–8).
3 Henry D. Inglis, *A journey throughout Ireland, 1834*, (2 vols., London, 1835), i, p. 334.

4   O.S. *Field name books, King's County*, vols.
    I & II, (1837–8).
5   N.L.I., Ms. 3521, Servants' wages account
    book of the Rev. Henry King, 1821–37.
6   Sir Charles Coote, *Statistical survey of the
    King's County*, (Dublin, 1801), p. 111.
7   Lewis, *Topographical dictionary*, i, p. iv.
8   Lewis, *Topographical dictionary*, i, p. 612.
9   N.L.I., Ms. 3551, Diary of Mrs. King,
    1838.
10 K.H. Connell, *The population of Ireland,
    1750–1845*, (Oxford, 1950), p. 3.
11 Joseph Lee, 'On the accuracy of the pre-
    Famine Irish censuses' in J.M. Goldstrom
    and L.A. Clarkson (eds.), *Irish population,
    economy and society*, (Oxford, 1981), p. 54.
12 *Poor inquiry (Ireland), Appendix (F)*, [38],
    H.C. 1836, xxxiii, 1, pp 82–5, and
    Appendix (D), [36], H.C. 1836, xxxi, 1,
    pp 83 & 85.
13 Connell, *Population of Ireland*, p. 27.
14 As in note 13, p. 44.
15 *Census of Ireland, 1831*, H.C. 1833, (254),
    xxxix, 1, p. 114–5, and *Census of Ireland,
    1841*, [504], H.C. 1843, xxiv, 1, pp 68–9.
16 *Poor Inquiry (Ireland), Appendix (E)*, [37],
    H.C. 1836, xxxii, 1, pp 82–5.
17 O.S. *Field name books, King's County*,
    (1837–8), Ballylin, vol. II, p. 768;
    Moystown, vol. II, p. 749; Clonbonniff,
    vol. II, p. 743.
18 T.W. Freeman, 'Land and people,
    c. 1841' in W.E. Vaughan, (ed.), *A new
    history of Ireland, V*, (Oxford, 1989), p. 253.
19 *Census of Ireland, 1841*, [504], H.C. 1843,
    xxiv, 1, p. 68.
20 Lewis, *Topographical dictionary*, ii, p. 225.
    See also, Coote, *Statistical survey of the
    King's County*, p. 19.
21 National Archives, O.P.K.C., 23 July 1839.
22 See Alan Everitt, 'Country, county and
    town: patterns of regional evolution in
    England' in *Transactions of Royal Historical
    Society*, 5th ser., xxix, (1979), p. 80.
23 N.L.I., Ms. 3551, Diary of Mrs. King, 1838.
24 As in note 23, 20 August 1838.
25 National Archives, O.P.K.C., 11 July
    1837, and *King's County Chronicle*, 31
    March, 1847.
26 *Poor inquiry (Ireland), Appendix (D)*, [36],
    H.C. 1836, xxxi, 1, p. 83.
27 *Poor inquiry (Ireland), Appendix (E)*, [37],
    H.C. 1836, xxxii, 1, p. 83.
28 As in note 27.
29 National Archives, O.P.K.C., 11 July 1837.

30 H.P.R. Finberg, 'Local history' in H.P.R.
    Finberg & V.H.T. Skipp, *Local history,
    objective and pursuit*, (Newton Abbot,
    1967), p. 33.
31 National Archives, O.P.K.C., 4 April
    1838; 22 August 1839; 28 August 1839;
    31 May 1839.
32 National Archives, O.P.K.C., 30 May 1838.
33 National Archives, O.P.K.C., 31 August
    1836.

THE KINGS OF BALLYLIN

1   Registry of Deeds, Book 214, p. 435, no.
    141733.
2   O.S., *Field name books, King's County*,
    vol. II, pp 766–80; The townlands are
    Aughaboy, Ballydaly, Ballylin, Ballyvlin,
    Ballyvora, Brehogue, Coole, Curragh-
    wheery, Derricabeg, Ferbane,
    Kilcolganbeg, Kilcolganmore, Kincor,
    Lisdermot and Wheery.
3   Letters to John and Henry King from
    Robert Jones Lloyd, who controlled 11
    townlands in Leitrim, are reproduced in
    F.S.L. Lyons, 'Vicissitudes of a middleman
    in Co. Leitrim, 1810–27' in *I.H.S.*, ix, no.
    25 (1955), pp 300–18.
4   As in note 2.
5   N.L.I., King Collection, P.C. 308–12. See
    also, R. J. Hayes, *Manuscript sources for the
    history of Irish civilisation*, (14 vols.,Boston,
    1965), viii, pp 227–51.
6   As in note 2.
7   *Poor inquiry (Ireland), Appendix (D)*, [36],
    H.C. 1836, xxxi, 1, pp 82–5.
8   *Poor inquiry (Ireland), supplement II to
    appendices (D)–(F), containing returns of
    civil bill ejectments, 1827–33*, [39], H.C.
    1836, xxxiv, 1, pp 96–107.
9   National Archives, O.P.K.C., 11 July 1837.
10 *Census of Ireland, 1851*, [1488], H.C.
    1852, xci, 129, p. 139.
11 N.L.I., King Collection, P.C. 308–12,
    folders 51–3.
12 N.L.I., King Collection, P.C. 308–12,
    folders 28 & 29.
13 N.L.I., Ms. 1421, Account book of
    Rev. H. King, 1835–52.
14 Richard Griffith, *Valuation of tenements*,
    (1854), vol. on King's County, p. 210.
15 *Poor inquiry, (Ireland), Appendix (F)*, [38],
    H.C. 1836, xxxiii, 1, p. 85.
16 As in note 15, p. 83.

17 Earl of Rosse, *Letters on the state of Ireland*, (London, 1847), p. 18.
18 *Poor inquiry (Ireland), Appendix (F)*, [38], H.C. 1836, xxxiii, 1, p. 83.
19 National Archives, O.P.K.C., 11 Sept. 1839.
20 N.L.I., King Collection, P.C. 308–12, lease between Rev. H. King and John English, May 1821.
21 N.L.I., King Collection, P.C. 308–12, leases between King and Horne, May 1821; Horne and Keating, 1825; surrender of lease between Horne and King, April 1832.
22 *Poor inquiry (Ireland), Supplement II to Appendices (D)–(F), containing returns of civil bill ejectments, 1827–33*, [39], H.C. 1836, xxxiv, 1, pp 96–107.
23 National Archives, O.P.K.C., 24 April 1838 & 14 April 1839.
24 N.L.I., Ms. 3551, Diary of Mrs. King, 1838.
25 N.L.I., King Collection, P.C. 308–12, lease between Henry King and Edward Carr and George Carr, May 1823; National Archives, O.P.K.C., 11 July 1837.
26 Lewis, *Topographical dictionary*, ii, p. 621.
27 Sir Charles Coote, *Statistical survey of the King's County*, (Dublin, 1801), pp 108 & 110.
28 N.L.I., King Collection, P.C. 308–12, folder 46.
29 N.L.I., Ms. 3551, Diary of Mrs. King, 17 Oct. & 15 Dec. 1838.
30 N.L.I., Ms. 3521, Servants' wages account book of Rev. H. King, 1821–37.
31 National Archives, O.P.K.C., 11 July 1837.
32 *Poor inquiry (Ireland), Appendix (D)*, [36], H.C. 1836, xxxi, 1, p. 85.
33 George Cornewall Lewis, *On local disturbances in Ireland*, (London, 1836), p. 298.
34 Mark Bence-Jones, *A guide to Irish country houses*, (Hampshire, 1988), p. 23.
35 N.L.I., Ms. 3551, Diary of Mrs. King, 6 Jan. 1839.
36 N.L.I., Ms. 3521, Servants' wages account book of the Rev. H. King, 1821–37.
37 N.L.I., Ms. 3551, Diary of Mrs. King, 1838.

ECONOMIC LIFE

1 *Census of Ireland, 1831*, H.C. 1833, (254), xxxix, pp 114–5 and *Census of Ireland, 1841*, [504], H.C. 1843, xxiv, pp 68–9.

2 Lewis; *Topographical dictionary*, (1837); O.S. *Field name books, King's County*, (1837–8).
3 As in note 1.
4 *Poor inquiry (Ireland), Appendix (D)*, [36], H.C. 1836, xxxi, 1, pp 82–5.
5 As in note 4, p. 83.
6 As in note 4, p. 85.
7 As in note 4, p. 83.
8 As in note 4, p. 85.
9 As in note 4, p. 83.
10 Sir Charles Coote, *Statistical survey of the King's County*, (Dublin, 1801), p. 103.
11 O.S., *Field name books, King's County*, vol. II, pp 542, 753 & 762.
12 See, Conrad Gill, *The rise of the Irish linen industry*, (Oxford, 1925), p. 127.
13 *Poor inquiry (Ireland), Appendix (E)*, [37], H.C. 1836, xxxii, 1, p. 83.
14 Tullamore Library, Grand Jury Presentment book, 1838.
15 See *Poor inquiry (Ireland), Appendix (F)*, [38], H.C. 1836, xxxiii, 1, pp 82–5.
16 As in note 15, pp 83, 84.
17 E. Wakefield, *An account of Ireland, statistical and political*, (London, 1812), pp 642–3, 651.
18 N.L.I., Ms. 3551, Diary of Mrs. King, 12 March 1838.
19 National Archives, O.P.K.C., 27 Feb. 1837 & 2 March 1839.
20 National Archives, O.P.K.C., 1835–40.
21 National Archives, O.P.K.C., 2 Aug. 1839.
22 See, *A history of Cloghan parish*, (Cloghan History Group), (Ferbane, 1988), pp 56–8.
23 N.L.I., King Collection P.C. 308–12, Christopher Dillon to Andrew Baggot, 30 Aug. 1825.
24 Coote, *Statistical survey of the King's County*, (Dublin 1801), p. 111.
25 Lewis, *Topographical dictionary*, i, p. 612, and *Report of the commissioners on the state of fairs and markets in Ireland*, [1647], H.C. 1852–3, xli, 79, pp 44 & 53.
26 *Returns showing the number of disturbances which have taken place in Ireland, during the years 1840–3, at the different fairs and markets, in the collection of tolls and customs*, H.C. 1843, (589), 1, 163, p. 13.
27 National Archives, O.P.K.C., 31 May 1839.
28 National Archives, O.P.K.C., 11 July 1837.
29 National Archives, O.P.K.C., 14 Nov. 1838.
30 N.L.I., Ms. 3551, Diary of Mrs. King, 2nd, 5th & 10th Oct. 1838.

31 National Archives, O.P.K.C., 9 Oct. 1838.
32 N.L.I., Ms. 3551, Diary of Mrs. King, 17 Oct. & 15 Dec. 1838.
33 N.L.I., Ms. 3521, Servants' wages account book of the Rev. H. King.
34 N.L.I., King Collection P.C. 308–12, receipts for 1835.
35 N.L.I., Ms. 3551, Diary of Mrs. King.
36 *Poor inquiry (Ireland), Appendix (E)*, [37], H.C. 1836, xxxii, I, pp 82–5.
37 Lewis, *Topographical dictionary*, i, p. 328.
38 As in note 36, p. 85.

POVERTY

1 *Poor inquiry, (Ireland), Appendix (E)*, [37], H.C. 1836, xxxii, I, p. 85.
2 See, T.P. O'Neill, 'The Catholic Church and the relief of the poor' in *Archivium Hibernicum*, xxxi, (1973), p. 134.
3 See, Helen Burke, *The people and the poor law in nineteenth century Ireland*, (Sussex, 1987), pp 14–20.
4 George Cornewall Lewis, *On local disturbances in Ireland*, (London, 1836), p. 321.
5 N.L.I., King Collection, P.C. 308–12, Edward Keogh, P.P. to King, 22 July 1830.
6 N.L.I., Ms. 3551, Diary of Mrs. King, 20 Aug. 1838.
7 *Census of Ireland, 1841*, [504], H.C. 1843, xxiv, I, pp 68–9.
8 *Poor inquiry (Ireland), Appendix (E)*, [37], H.C. 1836, xxxii, I, p. 82–5.
9 As in note 8.
10 *Poor inquiry (Ireland), Appendix (D)*, [36], H.C. 1836, xxxi, I, p. 85.
11 National Archives, O.P.K.C., 11 Sept. 1839.
12 *Poor inquiry (Ireland), Appendix (D)*, [36], H.C. 1836, xxxi, I, pp 82–5.
13 As in note 12, p. 85.
14 N.L.I., Ms. 3551, Diary of Mrs. King, 1838.
15 *Poor inquiry (Ireland), Appendix (E)*, [37], H.C. 1836, xxxii, I, pp 12–3.
16 *The Leinster Express* (Maryborough), 20 Jan. 1838.
17 *Poor inquiry (Ireland), Appendix (D)*, [36], H.C. 1836, xxxi, I, p. 83.
18 Lewis, *Topographical dictionary*, (1837), ii, p. 225.
19 *Poor inquiry (Ireland), Appendix (E)*, [37], H.C. 1836, xxxii, I, p. 83.
20 National Archives, O.P.K.C., 11 July 1837.

21 As in note 17.
22 Burke, *The people and the poor law*, p. 10.
23 *Poor inquiry (Ireland), Appendix (D)*, [36], H.C. 1836, xxxi, I, p. 83.
24 National Archives, O.P.K.C., 14 Dec. 1839.
25 *The Athlone Independent*, 6 Jan. 1836.
26 N.L.I., King Collection, P.C. 308–12, Edward Keogh P.P. to King, 22 July 1830
27 *Poor inquiry (Ireland), Appendix (F)*, [38], H.C. 1836, xxxiii, I, pp 82–5.
28 As in note 27, p. 84.
29 National Archives, O.P.K.C., 11 July 1837.
30 *Copies of the several documents . . . on which the barony of . . . Garrycastle . . . [was] declared to be in a state of disturbance and insubordination, 1834*, (241), xlvii, 431, p. 431.
31 Tullamore Library, Parsonstown Union Minute Book, June 1839–Jan. 1843, pp 32, 35 & 39.
32 As in note 31, pp 29–31 & 52.
33 See, Burke, *The people and the poor law*, p. 47.
34 *Poor inquiry (Ireland), Appendix (F)*, [38], H.C. 1836, xxxiii, I, p. 13.

CRIME

1 *Copies of the several documents . . . on which the baronies of Ballyboy, Ballybritt, Eglish and Garrycastle in the King's County were declared to be in a state of disturbance and insubordination, 1834*, (241) xlvii, 431.
2 As in note 1, pp 431 & 434.
3 George Cornewall Lewis, *On local disturbances in Ireland*, (London, 1836), pp 229–32.
4 *The state of Ireland since 1835, in respect of crime and outrage, which have rendered life and property insecure in that part of the Empire*, H.C. 1839, (486) xi, I, p. 526.
5 Galen Broeker, *Rural disorder and police reform in Ireland, 1812–36*, (London & Toronto, 1970), p. 11.
6 As in note 5, p. 206.
7 James W. O'Neill, 'A look at Captain Rock: agrarian rebellion in Ireland, 1815–45' in *Éire-Ireland*, xvii, no. 3 (1982), p. 28.
8 National Archives, O.P.K.C., 11 Feb. 1835; 31 Jan. 1837; 30 May 1837.
9 *Copies of the several documents . . . 1834*, (241) xlvii, 431, p. 436.

10 Joseph Lee, 'The Ribbonmen' in T.D. Williams (ed.), *Secret societies in Ireland,* (Dublin, 1973), p. 33.

11 Cornwall Lewis, *On local disturbances in Ireland,* p. 99.

12 National Archives, O.P.K.C., 12 Dec. 1835; 10 Mar. 1837; 4 Aug. 1839.

13 National Archives, O.P.K.C., 15 May 1836.

14 National Archives, O.P.K.C., 11 Feb. 1835; 6 Oct. 1835; 23 Mar. 1839.

15 National Archives, O.P.K.C., 11 July 1837.

16 National Archives, O.P.K.C., 28 Aug. 1839.

17 See, O'Neill, 'A look at Captain Rock', p. 18.

18 National Archives, O.P.K.C., 9 Jan. 1835; 16 Feb. 1837; 19 April 1837; 17 Oct. 1838.

19 National Archives, O.P.K.C., 19 Sept. 1838.

20 National Archives, O.P.K.C., 2 Nov, 1839; 21 Mar. 1836; 23 May & 14 June 1839; 22 Aug. 1835.

21 *Poor inquiry (Ireland), Appendix (E),* [37], H.C. 1836, xxxii, 1, pp 82–5.

22 National Archives, O.P.K.C., 25 June 1835 & 11 Oct. 1837.

23 National Archives, O.P.K.C., 24 Feb. 1839.

24 National Archives, O.P.K.C., 12 Feb. 1838 & 17 Dec. 1839.

25 National Archives, O.P.K.C., 9 Dec. 1838; 12 Oct. 1838; 9 May 1838.

26 *Returns . . . of the numbers of persons committed to the different gaols . . . for trial in the year 1835,* H.C. 1836, (97) xlvii, 379, pp 40–1; *1836,* H.C. 1837, (158) xlv, 225, pp. 38–9; *1837,* H.C. 1837–8, (208) xlvi, 251, pp 42–3; *1838,* H.C. 1839, (78) xxxviii, 649, pp 40–3; *1839,* H.C. 1840, (44) xxxviii, 453, pp 40–3; *1840,* H.C. 1841 Session 1, (101) xviii, 547, pp 40–3.

27 National Archives, O.P.K.C., 2 Jan. 1838.

28 Cornwall Lewis, *On local disturbances in Ireland,* p. 232, and; *Copies of the several documents . . . ,* H.C. 1834, (241) xlvii, 431, p. 435.

29 *Poor inquiry (Ireland), Appendix (E),* [37], H.C. 1836, xxxii, 1, pp 82–5.

30 National Archives, O.P.K.C., 19 July 1838; 1 May 1839; 13 April 1839; 23 Sept. 1839.

31 National Archives, O.P.K.C., 10 Sept. 1835 & 21 Feb. 1838.

32 See Cornwall Lewis, *On local disturbances in Ireland,* p. 232.

33 N.L.I., Ms. 3551, Diary of Mrs. King, 1838.

34 Gale E. Christianson, 'Secret societies and agrarian violence in Ireland, 1790–1840' in *Agricultural History,* xlvi, no. 4 (Oct. 1972), p. 372.

35 *Copies of the several documents . . . ,* 1834, (241) xlvii, 431, pp 431–6.

36 *Returns of all crimes and outrages . . . from the 1st Jan. 1836 to 12th Dec. 1837,* H.C. 1837–8, (157) xlvi, 427, p. 10.

37 National Archives, O.P.K.C., 27 Feb. 1837; 11 Feb. 1838; 7 April 1839.

38 National Archives, O.P.K.C., 21 Mar. 1837; 11 Feb. 1838; 11 Sept. 1839.

39 *Return of all rewards offered by proclamation of the Lord Lieutenant . . . from 1st Jan. 1836 to 12th Dec. 1837,* H.C. 1837–8, (157) xlvi, 427, pp 2–9.

40 National Archives, O.P.K.C., 3 May 1835.

41 *Copies of the several documents . . . , 1834,* H.C. (241) xlvii, 431, pp 432 & 436.

42 National Archives, O.P.K.C., 11 Mar. 1837.

43 As in note 41, p. 435.

44 As in note 41, pp 434 & 436.

45 *Returns of the courts of Petty Sessions . . . for the year ending 31st Dec. 1835,* 1836, (415) xlii, 463, p. 114.

46 As in note 41, p. 431 & 436.

47 *The state of Ireland since 1835 in respect of crime and outrage . . . , 1839,* (486) xi, 1, pp 446–7.

48 As in note 26, for the years 1835 & 1838.

49 National Archives, O.P.K.C., 9 Nov. 1835.

50 *Copies of the several documents . . . , 1834,* H.C. (241) xlvii, 431, pp 434 & 432.

51 As in note 50, p. 436.

52 Cornwall Lewis, *On local disturbances in Ireland,* pp 50ff., 321 & 90.

SOCIAL AFFAIRS

1 Mary E. Daly, *Social and economic history of Ireland since 1800,* (Dublin, 1981) p. 6.

2 N.L.I., King Collection P.C. 308–12, Thomas Wallace to King, 2 April 1827.

3 N.L.I., King Collection P.C. 308–12, Leitrim to King, 12 July 1830.

4 Lewis, *Topographical dictionary,* ii, pp 221–2.

5 National Archives, O.P.K.C., 19 May 1839.

6 *Athlone Conservative Advocate,* 20 July 1837.

7 *Dublin Evening Post*, 1 Aug. 1837.
8 See, T.P. O'Neill, 'The Catholic Church and the relief of the poor' in *Archivium Hibernicum*, xxxi, (1973), pp 132–45.
9 *Royal commission on the state of religious and other public instruction in Ireland; First report*, 1835, H.C. [45], xxxiii, 1, pp 166–7.
10 N.L.I., King Collection, P.C. 308–12, Keogh to King, 5 March 1830 & 22 July 1830.
11 National Archives, O.P.K.C., 29 Nov. 1837 & 18 July 1839.
12 National Archives, O.P.K.C., 18 Nov. 1838 & 1 Mar. 1839.
13 National Archives, O.P.K.C., 8 Aug. 1839; 26 April 1839 & 9 May 1839.
14 N.L.I., Ms. 3551, Diary of Mrs. King, 1838. Vestry or visitation records could not be located.
15 See, Desmond Bowen, *The Protestant crusade in Ireland, 1800–70*, (Dublin, 1978), p. 67.
16 As in note 14. Mrs. King's family had a history of dedication to evangelical causes. Her brother, John Lloyd of Birr, had acted as treasurer to a fund set up to build a new church during the 'Crotty Schism' in Birr in the 1820s. See, Baptist W. Noel, *Notes of a short tour through the midland counties of Ireland in the summer of 1836*, (London, 1837), pp 225–8.
17 Noel, *Notes on a short tour through the midland counties of Ireland*, pp 219–23.
18 *First report of the commissioners on education in Ireland*, H.C. 1825, (400), xii, pp 66 & 81.
19 *Royal commission on the state of religious and other public instruction in Ireland; Second report*, H.C. 1835, [47], xxxiv, pp 134, 148 & 167.
20 N.L.I., Ms. 3551, Diary of Mrs. King, 1838.
21 See, Donald H. Akenson, *The Irish education experiment, the national system of education in the 19th century*, (London and Toronto, 1970), pp 192–3; *Athlone Conservative Advocate*, 1 June 1837.

22 National Archives, ED1/47, no. 4; ED1/47, no. 106.
23 *Appendix to the fifth report of the commissioners of national education in Ireland*, H.C. 1839, (240) xvi, 341, pp 52–3.
24 Lewis, *Topographical dictionary*, ii, p. 225.
25 *Royal commission on state of religious and other public instruction in Ireland, Second report*, H.C. 1835, [47], xxxiv, 1, pp 159, 161 & 167.
26 *Census of Ireland*, 1841, [504], H.C. 1843, xxiv, 1, pp 68–9.
27 National Archives, O.P.K.C., 11 March 1837.
28 Lewis, *Topographical dictionary*, ii, p. 225.
29 As in note 25.
30 N.L.I., Ms. 3551, Diary of Mrs. King, 1838, and; Ms. 3526, Commonplace book of Harriet King, 1839.
31 See, Owen G. Harry, 'The Hon. Mrs. Ward (1827–69), artist, naturalist, astronomer and Ireland's first lady of the microscope' in *The Irish Naturalists' Journal*, xxi, no. 5, (Jan. 1984), pp 193–200.
32 N.L.I., Ms. 3551, Diary of Mrs. King, 11 Oct. 1838.
33 N.L.I., Ms. 3551, Diary of Mrs. King, 1838.
34 N.L.I., King Collection, P.C. 308–12, letter to King 2 July 1830; National Archives, O.P.K.C., 14 Dec. 1839.
35 Lewis, *Topographical dictionary*, ii, p. 222.
36 Tullamore Library, Grand Jury Presentment book, 1838.
37 N.L.I., Ms. 3551, Diary of Mrs. King, 1838.
38 *Poor inquiry (Ireland), Appendix (D)*, [36], H.C. 1836, xxxi, 1, p. 83.
39 National Archives, O.P.K.C., 26 Sept. 1838; 18 July 1839; 27 Sept. 1839.

CONCLUSION

1 Patrick Kavanagh, 'The parish and the universe' in *Collected Pruse*, (sic), (London, 1973), p. 283.